GODDING

GODDING

Human Responsibility and the Bible

Virginia Ramey Mollenkott

CROSSROAD · NEW YORK

1987

The Crossroad Publishing Company
370 Lexington Avenue, New York, N.Y. 10017

Printed in the United States of America

Library of Congress Cataloging in Publication Data

Mollenkott, Virginia R.
   Godding: human responsibility and the Bible.

   1. Christian life—1960–   2. Responsibility.
3. Incarnation.   4. Feminism—Religious aspects—
Christianity.   5. Sex—Religious aspects—Christianity.
6. Race discrimination—Religious aspects—Christianity.
7. Arms race—Religious aspects—Christianity.   I. Title.
BV4501.2.M553   1987   248.4   86–29219
ISBN 0–8245–0824–6

ACKNOWLEDGMENTS

Grateful acknowledgment is made to the publishers for
permission to reprint the following poems:
   "Coal" by Audre Lorde. Reprinted from *Coal*, poems by Audre Lorde,
by permission of W. W. Norton & Company, Inc. Copyright © 1968, 1970, 1976
by Audre Lorde.
   "Sojourn in the Whale" by Marianne Moore. Reprinted with
permission of Macmillan Publishing Company from *Collected Poems*
of Marianne Moore. Copyright 1935 by Marianne Moore, renewed 1963
by Marianne Moore and T. S. Eliot.
   "Whirlwind Courtship" by Thomas John Carlisle. Reprinted from *Journey
with Job* by Thomas John Carlisle, © 1976 by Wm. B. Eerdmans
Publishing Co. Used by permission of the publisher.

BIBLE VERSIONS USED

AILL A, B, C	*An Inclusive Language Lectionary: Readings for Year A* (1983), *Year B* (1984), *Year C* (1985). Published in three volumes by John Knox Press (Atlanta) Pilgrim Press (New York), and Westminster Press (Philadelphia)
NIV	*The New International Version* (1978)
RSV	Revised Standard Version (1952)

For all my sisters of every place and time
who have been stepped on by patriarchal feet
but nevertheless have been sustained, embraced,
and filled by God . . .

And for my brothers who have identified themselves
with those who have been stepped on . . .

That we may empower one another for the joy
and responsibility of godding.

God is over all things, under all things;
outside all; within but not enclosed;
without but not excluded; above but not
raised up; below but not depressed; wholly above,
presiding; wholly beneath, sustaining;
wholly without, embracing; wholly within,
filling.

—Hildebert, Archbishop
of Tours, c. 1125

Contents

1

The Nature of Godding

The Bible never ceases to amaze me. Take, for instance, the remarks of Jesus to his disciples in Matthew 5:43–45:

> You have heard that it was said, "You shall love your neighbor and hate your enemy." But I say to you, love your enemies and pray for those who persecute you, so that you may be children of [God] your [Mother and] Father who is in heaven; for God makes the sun rise on the evil and on the good, and sends rain on the just and on the unjust. (AILL A)

In these comments Jesus implies that God's behavior is intended as a model for human behavior. Because God gives sunshine and rain without discriminating between just and unjust people, those who wish to be known as God's children are instructed to love and pray for their acquaintances without discriminating between friends and enemies. Jesus even implies that it is precisely *through* loving our enemies and praying for those who persecute us that we become God's children! I do not see this as a contradiction of the concept of salvation by grace through faith. Instead, I read this as a gloss upon it, an explanation of the familial resemblance that develops as the evidence of at-one-ment with God.

Here and elsewhere, Jesus implies that his disciples are expected to pattern their relationship after God's behavior in a mirroring process ("as in heaven, so on earth"), and that the mirroring of unconditional love is the sign of membership in the faith-family of God. This human embodiment of God's

1

universal concern is surely one of the meanings of the prayer Jesus taught us to pray: "Your will be done on earth as it is in heaven." Apart from miracles, how would God's will be done on earth, if not through human agency?

What I am driving at is simple enough, and is the thesis of this book: that human responsibility, in its deepest and fullest dimension, entails *godding*, an embodiment or incarnation of God's love in human flesh, with the goal of cocreating with God a just and loving human society. I think 1 John 4:16–17 is a passage about godding:

God is love; and [the one who] abides in love abides in God, and God abides in [that one]. In this is love perfected with us, that we may have confidence for the day of judgment, *because as [God] is, so are we in this world.* (RSV, emphasis and inclusive language mine)

GODDING: A POET'S PERSPECTIVE (1789)

In 1789 the great English poet William Blake published a poem entitled "The Divine Image," describing in eighteenth-century language the phenomenon this book has termed *godding*:

To Mercy, Pity, Peace, and Love
All pray in their distress;
And to these virtues of delight
Return their thankfulness.

For Mercy, Pity, Peace, and Love
Is God, our Father dear,
And Mercy, Pity, Peace, and Love
Is Man, his child and care.

For Mercy has a human heart
Pity a human face,
And Love, the human form divine,
And Peace, the human dress.

Then every man, of every clime,
That prays in his distress
Prays to the human form divine,
Love, Mercy, Pity, Peace.

And all must love the human form,
In heathen, turk, or jew;
Where Mercy, Love, and Pity dwell
There God is dwelling too.

Like Jesus, Blake locates the human presence of God in *relationship*, in *caring*. In order to break down the human tendency to categorize people as "us" or "them" (loving those close to us and hating our "enemies"), Blake mentions three groups that were either foreign or feared in eighteenth-century Britain: heathen people, Turkish people, and Jewish people. They too, have the human form divine, Blake says, inasmuch as they too are capable of Mercy, Love, and Pity; hence these divine capacities must be loved in them as much as in others more familiar to us. When we acknowledge Mercy, Love, Peace, and Pity in those we have termed the other or the enemy, then our own Mercy, Love, Peace, and Pity are stimulated, and the result is peace within our whole environment. Godding, Blake implies, is the path to peace. To acknowledge God's presence in the Mercy, Love, Peace, and Pity of our enemies is to exercize or embody God's presence in ourselves as well. The human bonding of God's presence in us and in them is a bonding called peace.

WHAT GODDING IS NOT

Godding is the very opposite of lording it over other people. Where each person is equally made in God's image, the relationship that suggests itself is one of mutual service, support, and caring. God's presence is known in those relationships that are mutually sympathetic, helpful, and interdependent rather than in hierarchical one-up, one-down relationships. The goal here is not to get into a game of "I am godding better than you," but rather to grow intentionally toward the recognition of God's image in everyone and in everything, and toward the mutual respect that such recognition entails. Since Scripture assures us that God is "above all and through all, and in you all" (Eph. 4:6), we need not fear to acknowledge a divine milieu.

Nor need we fear to acknowledge God's presence within ourselves, in one sense communicating with us in the depth of our spirit, and in another sense fully identified with us. God is *both* "other" *and* ourselves, more fully ourselves than our superficial body-identified personalities could ever be, and yet beyond us, more all-encompassing than we could imagine Her to be, more mysterious than any of His names!

To recognize that God is becoming God's Self through the process of my living is emphatically not the same as worshiping myself. To worship myself would be to make the very stupid mistake of assuming that one aspect of an enormously complex being or process is the entire being or process. I really *am* one embodiment or manifestation or incarnation of God, but I am not God. I am part of that "all" that God is "above," and "in," and "through," but my infinitesimal parameters do not contain the whole of who God is. And yet they *do*, in the sense that God is completely present at every point. Like the black women in *For Colored Girls Who Have Considered Suicide When the Rainbow Is*

Enuf, "I found God in myself/And I loved her/I loved her fiercely."

IS MONOTHEISM THE ENEMY OF PLURALISM?

Throughout history, monotheism has caused countless wars and millions of deaths; so it would be easy to blame the concept of "one God only" for many of the world's ills. It would be easy to assume that monotheism is the antithesis of pluralism, and hence antithetical to a democratic society like America's, in which no particular political, ideological, cultural, or ethnic group is automatically and permanently dominant. (The philosophical categories of monism versus pluralism also give rise to the assumption that monotheism is the antithesis of democratic pluralism). However, the problem stems not from monotheism itself, but from the arrogant notion that any person or any religious group knows all there is to know about the one God.

Viewed from a more biblical perspective, the concept of one Source affirms rather than denies pluralism. If creation contains the infinite variety that it obviously does contain, and yet stems from a single source and is energized by one single Spirit, then we must conclude that the one Source and the one Energy (God or the Spirit of God) has a powerful preference for pluralism!

I used to suspect that God was very prideful when I read such passages as "I am the Sovereign, that is my name; my glory I give to no other, nor my praise to graven images" (Isa. 42:8, AILL B). I thought that remark sounded a whole lot like a cosmic bully shouting "*Me*! First, last, and always, *me*!" But if God is indeed *above* all and *through* all and *in* all, then the statement takes on a very different meaning. God is insisting on our attention to all—to the whole—to the entire being and becoming of time and eternity, as opposed to our focusing on any one segment or particle of it. The nature of graven images is that they are specific and concrete and therefore limited to one particular facet of the universe. God will not stand for elevating any single facet of Herself into the whole who She is; His glory He will give to no other because to do so would be to mistake one aspect for the whole vast structure and process of reality. That is why to worship myself or make myself normative for other people would not only be stupid; it would also be the sin of idolatry. That's also why I dare not elevate the doctrines, ideas, and practices of my own religion into a position of power over other religions. I dare not extract any one thing from the context of the whole field in which God is above, through, and in everything and everyone. Godding is a humbling experience because it makes me aware that I am only one manifestation among infinite millions of manifestations. Yet godding is also empowering because I am a manifestation of *God*. God Herself! God Himself! God Itself! Above all. Through all. And in us all.

WHO IS GOD'S RIGHTEOUS SERVANT?

The Hebrew prophet Isaiah provides a description of God's righteous servant, a person who is devoted to godding:

Behold my servant, whom I uphold, my chosen, in whom my soul delights; I have put my Spirit upon my servant who will bring forth justice to the nations.... My servant will not fail or be discouraged till justice has been established in the earth.... Thus says God, the Sovereign One, who created the heavens and stretched them out, who spread forth the earth and what comes from it, who gives breath to the people upon it and spirit to those who walk in it: "I am the Sovereign One, I have called you in righteousness, I have taken you by the hand and kept you; I have given you as a covenant to the people, a light to the nations, to open the eyes that are blind, to bring out prisoners from the dungeon, from the prison those who sit in gloom." (Isa. 42:1–4, AILL B)

Traditionally, Jewish scholars have understood the "servant" to be a personification of the Hebrew nation. Traditionally, Christian scholars have understood the "servant" to be Jesus of Nazareth, the Christ or Messiah of God.[1] I would like to suggest that *both* of these understandings are too narrow. The traditional Jewish interpretation of the righteous servant tends to excuse people of other nations from their obligation to do justice, love mercy, and walk humbly with their God. The traditional Christian interpretation of the righteous servant tends to spotlight Jesus of Nazareth as a one-time-only phenomenon, someone out of the past at whose feet we may happily and lazily grovel, someone who will rescue us single-handedly and who thus relieves us of our contemporary responsibility to struggle to bring forth justice in our world. At the same time, the traditional Christian interpretation condemns to hell all those who do not understand the righteous servant to refer exclusively to Jesus the Messiah; instead of encouraging us to do justice and love mercy, this interpretation supports anti-Semitism, Christian triumphalism, and human divisiveness in general.

If both the traditional Jewish and Christian interpretations of the righteous servant seem too narrow, who then *is* this servant? The Epistle of James (2:5–9, 12–17) gives us some assistance. James tells us that God has chosen those who are poor in the eyes of the world to be rich in faith. James also reminds us that the sovereign law of Scripture is that we must love our neighbors as we love ourselves. He insists that economic elitism is a sin against this sovereign law, so that there will be no mercy for those who have not shown mercy in the use of their material resources. Specifically, James instructs us that it is not enough to wish our sisters and brothers well without actively sharing with them the necessities to meet their bodily needs. If faith does not translate into action, James says, it is simply dead; by contrast, he implies, those whose faith *does* undergird their practical outreach to help their sisters and brothers are those who are rich in faith and chosen of God. In other words, those who love their neighbors as they love themselves are "a covenant to the people, a light to the nations," opening eyes that are blind, bringing captives out of prison, out of the gloomy dungeons. Those who love their neighbors as they love themselves are corporately the righteous servant of God. They are "godders."

The righteous servant described by Isaiah is not only the personification of a Hebrew nation and not only Jesus of Nazareth as the Christ or Messiah of God, but also all human beings on the face of the earth who love their neighbor as they love themselves in a practical and active attempt to share the good basics of life. To use Christian terminology, we human beings are intended to function as a *corporate* Messiah of God, as "Christed Ones" or "little Christs" growing up into the Head, or Source, as the Christians at Ephesus were encouraged to do in Ephesians 4:15.

When we speak of becoming "Christed" we use Christian terminology. But we err whenever we unconsciously assume that the terms of one religion exclude from the the experience being described all people who would not use the same terminology. The experience of godding, which is a spiritual matter of the attitudes that are expressed in human relationships, is open to people of every religion. Across the face of the earth are people of various religions who would use different terms for those who love their neighbors as they love themselves and whose faith is alive because it leads to practical and structural acts of mercy. They, too, are members of the New Humanity. In the Apostle Paul's Christian terminology, all those who do justice and love mercy are "in Christ"; in Isaiah's Hebrew terminology, they become the "righteous servant of God." In the terms of Psalm 72, they are the people who have been endowed with God's own justice, who will to the full extent of their influence "deal justice to the poor and suffering." To do justice to the poor means working toward supplying their needs, out of recognition of their honorable status as the children of God. Doing justice means embodying mercy to outcast people—and even to the outcast or rejected aspects of our own beings!

BUT WHAT ABOUT THE UNIQUENESS OF JESUS CHRIST?

I am aware that what I have written may seem to some readers to be a denial of Jesus' uniqueness as the only Savior of the world, and therefore heresy. After all, Matthew's Gospel depicts Jesus as saying that anyone who denies Jesus on earth will be denied by Jesus in the presence of God in heaven, while anyone who acknowledges Jesus on earth will be acknowledged in heaven. And that has often been understood to mean that anyone who fails to acknowledge Jesus Christ as the one and only Savior of the world is lost forever, doomed to eternal death. But I do not believe that this acknowledgment of Jesus means that only Christians are acceptable to God. Jesus himself told us a parable that undercuts any such notion: the parable of the tax collector who went up into the temple to pray, and dared not raise his eyes, but simply cried out for God's mercy on his sinfulness. Jesus said, "this man went down to his house justified" (Luke 18:14). The tax collector knew nothing of salvation through Christ, and the fact that Jesus himself says the tax collector was justified constitutes proof for Christians that God has methods of justification that go beyond Christian boundaries.

Hence the acknowledgment of Jesus on earth does not mean that only Christians are capable of godding, of being God's righteous agents upon the earth. Acknowledging Jesus means living the life of Jesus as members of the New Humanity, as citizens of the New Creation, transformed by faith into new creatures who are empowered by God's grace to love our neighbors as we love ourselves. Acknowledging Jesus also means recognizing and acting out of our oneness with our Source, the Holy Spirit of the One God, just as Jesus recognized his oneness with the same Source and prayed that we also would be one as he was one with God (John 17:21). To be one with God means to recognize our oneness with all those who also have derived their being from the same Source: Muslims; Jews; post-Christian or post-Jewish feminists; gay people or heterosexual people; liberal or fundamentalist people; communist or capitalist people; black, white, red, or yellow people.

Acknowledging Jesus does not mean worshiping Jesus so much as worshiping the God whom Jesus worshiped and embodying the God whom Jesus embodied. As Jesus himself put it, "anyone who receives you receives me, and anyone who receives me receives God who sent me" (Matt. 10:40, AILL A). Jesus was talking to ordinary human beings when he said that, to his very ordinary disciples. Because they followed him, to receive them was to receive Jesus, and to receive Jesus was to receive his Source. In Hebrew terminology, to receive the righteous servant is to receive the Source of the righteous servant.

So yes, indeed, Jesus of Nazareth was the righteous servant of God, a Hebrew of the Hebrews in whom there was no guile, a liberator of captives and a healer of the blind and a light to the nations. But we also are called to be the righteous servant of God, the one who beacons to the nations the Good

News that "mercy triumphs over judgment." We are reminded that there is a profound reward for anyone who learns to see in a thirsty person with AIDS the very presence of the Holy One, and gives a cup of cold water simply because to help that person with AIDS is to help Jesus, and to help Jesus is to help the One who sent Jesus. It is not enough to say that the righteous servant of God is someone who lived and died and rose again two thousand years ago; many who have called Jesus "Lord, Lord" have failed to love their neighbors as they love themselves, and in Jesus' name have attacked and sometimes killed Jews and Muslims, gay people, people of other races, and people with physical limitations. To acknowledge Jesus before people is to use our energy in the service of justice and mercy.

NOT DOGMAS BUT DOINGS

Who, then, is the righteous servant of God? Who is the Body of Christ in this world? Who is engaged in godding? We will recognize these people not by their dogmas, but by their doings; not by their religious terms, but by their loyalty to all that Jesus and other righteous servants of God believed and practiced.

All of us—especially you, whoever you are as you read this book—all of us are invited to devote ourselves to the lifestyle of godding. In the words of Isaiah, our invitation reads:

> I am the Sovereign One, I have called you
>   in righteousness,
> I have taken you by the hand and kept you;
> I have given you as a covenant to the people,
>   a light to the nations,
>   to open the eyes that are blind,

> to bring out prisoners from the dungeon,
> from the prison those who sit in gloom.

R.S.V.P.

NOTES

1. *The Bible Reader: An Interfaith Interpretation*, ed. Walter M. Abbott, S.J., Rabbi Arthur Gilbert, Rolf Lanier Hunt, and J. Carter Swain (New York: Bruce Books, 1969), p. 435.

2

Job's Godding and Job's Repentance

Among the heroes of the Hebrew Scriptures, if ever there was a person wholly committed to godding, it was Job. His story is exceedingly important to our study because it illustrates several points: first, that our understanding of God's nature will have a great deal to do with our own joy and our sensitivity to others in our lives, no matter how righteous we may be; second, that in our attempts to "god" in the world we inhabit, it is absolutely vital that we stick to the truth of our own experience, refusing to temper our first-hand knowledge with pious platitudes or theories; and third, that dualistic categories are deadly to our thinking, feeling, and living. I will discuss the Book of Job in detail, partly because it has been widely misinterpreted, but mainly because it is highly relevant to our topic.

OF WHAT CAN A PERFECT PERSON REPENT?

From both the literary and theological perspectives, the big question concerning the Book of Job is this: Of what does Job repent? The narrator opens the book with the assurance that Job was "blameless and upright," a person who "feared God and turned away from evil" (1:1). We need go no farther than the word "blameless" to know that we are reading

but Job says everything of this

symbolic, stylized fiction, a philosophical fable or parable,[1] not a literal biography. But Isaac Asimov is surely correct that the religious and ethical meaning of the Book of Job would be the same even if it were historical rather than fictional.[2]

Should we be tempted to doubt the narrator's assessment of Job's virtue, it is borne out by God's own words in the dialogue with Satan (1:8). Even the Adversary is unable to fault Job's behavior, and therefore wishes to probe deeper, to get at Job's motives. Job's assessment of his own righteousness, detailed in chapter 31 but implicit everywhere, is never refuted. In fact, after the tremendous voice of God speaks from the whirlwind, God affirms Job's truthfulness to Eliphaz: "My wrath is kindled against you and against your two friends; for you have not spoken of me what is right, as my servant Job has" (42:7). So we really ought to be astonished when we hear Job, this blameless and upright human being who "godded" all his life, declare that "I despise myself,/and repent in dust and ashes" (42:6). *Repent?* Of *what?*

Bernhard W. Anderson, who identifies Job's repentance as "the key to the Book of Job," argues that Job is guilty of the "sin of self-sufficiency." Indeed, Anderson compares him to Prometheus, for Job is "a titanic figure who doubts, rebels, and shouts defiance at God." The fact that this same Job is also *vindicated by God* seems to elude Anderson, who sees Job's repentance as a conversion from self-sufficiency "into a relationship of personal trust and surrender."[3] Whereas most critics read God's speech from the whirlwind as making no reference to Job's guilt or lack of it, Anderson reads Yahweh's series of ironical questions as an overwhelming reminder that the creature *must* glorify the Creator, and therefore as a direct rebuke to Job's Promethean defiance.

James S. Ackerman agrees, pointing to Job 31:37 as an expression of Job's "tragic flaw." In that passage Job asserts: "I would give [God] an account of all my steps;/ like a prince I would approach [God]." Ackerman says that Job:

feels that the quality of his life has made him almost equal to God.... has put God under an obligation ... to admit that Job is righteous and to explain why he has suffered. If faith is the acceptance of God on [God's] own terms, then the author seems to be saying that Job's morality has destroyed his faith.[4]

According to Ackerman, Job is able to repent of his demands for a righteous God only after he has experienced a loving God. Ackerman claims that the second speech of God from the whirlwind shows Job that despite the mystery and agony of the universe, God nevertheless cares for humankind. Job therefore repents of his own feelings of self-sufficiency and self-righteousness, feelings he has perceived as the cause of his former alienation from God.

Other critics define the sin of which Job repents in a variety of ways, some of them anti-Semitic in tone if not in intention. It is one thing for eighteenth-century artist William Blake to portray Job as devoted to the law rather than to the spirit, so that his repentance signifies a rejection of his own legalism.[5] It is quite another thing for a twentieth-century critic to call the Book of Job a "forceful challenge to Judaism's legalistic framework," in which Job's repentance is tantamount to a repudiation of Jewish legalism, which is in turn identified as "the final expression of human pride, that righteous men could have an objective standard by which to hold God accountable."[6] Fortunately, most critics are more responsible, noting that the Hebrew Scriptures contain a *succession* of attitudes concerning human suffering and human righteousness. Harry Emerson Fosdick, for instance, sees Job as representing the viewpoint of later Judaism, that all trouble is *not* a penalty for wickedness, whereas Job's friends cling to earlier orthodoxies about punitive suffering.[7]

Like Ackerman, Georg Fohrer accuses Job of Promethean, heretical defiance of God; thus Job's repentance consists of learning that although suffering is mysterious and inscrutable, it is meaningful because of fellowship with the God whose action has (for whatever reason) caused the suffering.[8] Richard B. Sewall accuses Job of an "obsessive egotism (like Lear's or Ahab's)."[9] And Buckner Trawick sees Job's repentance as a belated recognition of his own insignificance: "to dare to question the purposes of the Almighty is pride of the most presumptuous sort."[10]

I know of no one who has achieved anything like Job's level of incorruptible, unwavering focus on reality, and I cannot help wondering what such critics think of *themselves* when the agonies of life force them to ask themselves difficult questions. Obviously, those who commit themselves to godding are vulnerable to all sorts of attacks from those who observe their struggles!

Joyce Vedral implies support for those critics who see Behemoth and Leviathan, the two primeval creatures mentioned in Job 40 and 41, as symbols of self-will and self-love, respectively. So Vedral concludes that "when Job despises himself and repents in dust and ashes, it is because he sees that through sufferings God seeks to reveal and remove these hidden monsters from his life."[11] Whatever has become of the narrator's and God's assessment of Job as blameless and upright?

Other critics are milder in their understanding of Job's repentance. To Robert Pfeifer, what Job learns is that his own miseries, like everyone else's, may have an incomprehensible purpose in the scheme of things. Or, if that is not true, they are "so infinitesimal in the cosmos that they hardly mar the perfection of God's creation and the character of the Creator."[12] Leland Ryken sees Job as repenting not of a specific moral sin, but simply because his view of God has been inadequate.[13] Issac Asimov connects Job's repentance to his realization of the folly of trying to penetrate God's plans and purposes with the limited mind of a human being.[14] Along similar lines, Samuel Sandmel sees Job as longing to understand, and even to litigate, that which cannot humanly be understood.[15] Job's repentance would therefore entail a long-overdue acceptance of human limitation.

Regardless of how severe a critic's judgment of Job's shortcoming may be, any assignment of moral fault to Job contradicts the narrator's repeated statement that Job is blameless, Job's own self-evaluation, God's evaluation at both the beginning and end of the book, and even the Adversary's (Satan's) evaluation of Job's behavior and attitudes. According to them all, Job is an excellent example of godding; yet he repents of *something*; and, as we have seen, the answers differ concerning what that something may have been.

PROSE PROLOGUE AND EPILOGUE VERSUS POETRY AT THE HEART: TWO DIFFERENT JOBS?

We must now ask ourselves this question: what is it about this work of literature that makes it possible for intelligent, sensitive readers to set their interpretations in contradiction to the facts of the story? The answer lies in the critical assumption that the prose Prologue (1:1–2:13) and Epilogue (42:7–17) are restatements of a very ancient and somewhat primitive legend, whereas the poetic dialogues (chapters 3 through 42:6) are the work of a much more profound and sophisticated author. The Job who struggles, protests, and finally repents "is not the improbable hero of the older tale, but a man of flesh and blood."[16] According to this view, there are really two Jobs: the inhumanly patient man of the legend (that is, of the Prologue and the Epilogue) and the passionately involved man of faith in the poetry at the heart of the book.

Certainly the concept of two different Jobs has much to recommend it. In the first place, it relieves the reader of having to figure out what a flawless human being might find in himself to despise. One is free to pass negative judgments on Job's tormented thrashings, and thus to trace improvements in his outlook. Furthermore, no one can seriously question that the legend of Job is considerably older than the book itself. Along with Noah and Daniel, Job is mentioned as a man of tremendous faith in Ezekiel 14:14 and 20, indicating that Job's status was already established by the time of the Exile (mid sixth century B.C.), a century or two before the Book of Job was written.

It is also undeniable that the Prologue takes a somewhat detached, impersonal attitude toward the experiment that will mean so much suffering for Job, whereas the poetic dialogues capture the anguish of the sufferer. The real question, however, is not whether there is a change of tone—certainly there *is*—but whether the switch from a universal, overarching point of view in the Prologue to an intensely subjective point of view in the poetry can justify the claim that "the Dialogue . . . confronts us with an altogether different Job."[17] If indeed the Job of the poetic discussion is "altogether different," then the perfection stated in the Prologue and Epilogue need not govern our understanding of the greater part of the book, including the tale of Job's repentance. But it is also reasonable to assume, as I do, that the author of Job has deliberately and successfully used the ancient legend as a frame for his poetry, shifting from an objective "eternal" point of view in the Prologue to a personally involved point of view in the poetry, with an appropriate shift of tone to match. If my assumption is correct, we are presented with the same Job seen from two perspectives: first the calm eternal perspective and then the chaotic temporal perspective. We are intended to view the temporal chaos without ever forgetting the glimpse we have received of that other dimension.

And we must be governed throughout by the insight that Job is blameless.

In addition to the external evidence concerning an ancient Job legend, the shift from prose to poetry, and the shifts in point of view and tone, several other factors also indicate that the author of Job has adapted an extant folktale as a prose framework for his poetry. The prose uses the divine name Yahweh, whereas the poetry uses El, Eloah, Elohim, and Shaddai. The Adversary, Accusor, or Prosecutor (Satan), who is clearly an agent of Yahweh, appears only in the Prologue. The Epilogue places responsibility for Job's misfortunes on God alone (42:11), and the poetry never suggests the presence of a Satan. Thus, the Book of Job hints broadly that Satan is to be understood as part of God's all-encompassing nature.

Above all, in the prose narrative Job is scrupulous, perhaps even obsessive, about observing the laws of purification. It was his regular custom to sacrifice burnt offerings for each of his children just in case they might secretly have cursed God in their hearts (1:5). Yet in the poetry, where Job spends all of chapter 31 describing his own righteous behavior, he never mentions his devotion to the rites of sacrifice.[18] Except for his avoidance of idolatry, Job's entire focus is on his ethical behavior toward other human beings and toward the earth. This indeed shows a major discrepancy between the ancient legend's characterization of Job and the character envisioned by the post-Exilic poet. Nevertheless, although their understandings of perfection differ, both the ancient legend and the poetic adapter depict Job as perfect.

Job's poetic vindications of his behavior in chapter 31 and elsewhere simply corroborate what is said in the Prologue and Epilogue. Although God insists that Job must answer to the One whom Job has accused, at no point does God charge Job with wrongdoing. Even the contemptuous question that people seem to apply to Job is perhaps not concerned with

Job at all. In 38:2, when God speaks out of the whirlwind, God's first words are "Who is this that darkens counsel by words without knowledge?" Almost all critics assume that God here refers to *Job* as speaking beyond his knowledge, because the next words are certainly addressed to Job ("Gird up your loins like a man;/ I will question you, and you shall declare to me") and because Elihu's speech is thought to be a later interpolation. But when we respond to the book as it has been handed down to us, we see that at the time of God's intervention, Job has been silent for six long chapters. It is *Elihu* who has been holding forth; and it is Elihu, not Job, whom God accuses of obscuring truth by speaking words without knowledge. And because Elihu is very impressed with his own wisdom and very intent on defending God's good name, we are expected to enjoy the irony that God professes not to remember Elihu's name ("Who *is* this?"). By contrast, God twice urges Job to brace himself for the series of unanswerable questions God is about to raise. For the Creator to expend so much energy upon one single creature seems a very great sign of respect.

A WHOLISTIC READING OF THE BOOK OF JOB

Ernest Wright, Reginald Fuller, and Eugene Goodheart all comment that the entire Book of Job rests on the presupposition that Job is a perfect or blameless man.[19] Obviously, I agree. And that forces upon me the responsibility of answering the question with which we began: If Job is blameless, of what does he repent?

Job repents of assuming himself to be a person separate from the One Person in the universe: the One who undergirds all personhood and encompasses the entire structure and process of reality. "I had heard of thee by the hearing of the ear," Job says; that is, he had understood God to be the Totally Other, the objectified Other who could be appeased by sacrifice and pleased by righteous dealings, in whose courtroom one's case could be argued. "But now my eye sees thee," Job continues; "therefore I despise myself, and repent in dust and ashes." What Job despises is the ego that could have imagined itself as a subject placating or accusing an objectified God. To see God is to recognize oneself as part of the process and structure of reality which we call by the name of God. To see God is to recognize the One whose name is "I AM WHO I AM" (Exodus 3:14). To see God is to despise the deluded, fragmented, separated ego that could think itself disconnected from the all-encompassing One. Nothing on earth is the equal of this One (41: 33), for if the whole is greater than the sum of its parts, certainly it is folly for any one of the parts to imagine itself outside of and equal to that which created and supports its being. "Who has given to me, that I should repay him?" asks the One whose Being undergirds everyone and everything. The question is rhetorical, of course, and in his wisdom Job does not try to answer it.

From the beginning, Job has been very clear about his oneness with other human beings. He had always been good to his servants because he understood that the same God who formed him had also formed them (31:13–15). He had treated fatherless young people as if he himself were their father; he knows that if he had raised his arm against them, he would have broken his own arm (31:21–22). But although Job is aware that the breath in his nostrils is God's breath (27:3), still he tends to see God as over against himself, as someone who has denied him justice (27:2), as somebody other, somebody opposite who has wronged him (19:6). Therefore Job wishes that God were literally a man like himself, so that they could confront each other in court (9:32). Knowing that wish to be futile, Job wishes that there were someone to arbitrate between the divine and the human person, an umpire "who might lay his hand upon us both," who would take away God's rod so that dread would no longer overwhelm him (9:33–35).

THE DUALISM OF JOB AND HIS FRIENDS

Although he has rejected the dogmatic platitudes of his friends and has correctly identified the reason for their dogmatism ("you see my calamity, and are afraid," 6:21), nevertheless Job is thinking within a dualistic category similar to theirs. God is on one side, humankind on the other. If suffering is not the fault of one, it must certainly be the fault of the other. The friends try to defend God's good name by accusing Job of some secret wrongdoing that has brought suffering upon him. Job knows that he has not sinned; and within his dualistic system there is only one alternative: he is forced to accuse God of wrongdoing.

What Job has in common with his friends is the dualistic polarization of creature versus Creator. This is not a moral fault, for Job is blameless. But it is an erroneous pattern of thought that causes Job a great deal of grief.

Knowing himself to be innocent, Job in his agony wonders whether God is deriving pleasure from spurning him and smiling upon the wicked (10:3). Even before his troubles, Job has the courage and honesty to recognize that the same God who gives pleasure also gives pain: he asks his wife, "Shall we accept good from God, and not trouble?" (1:10). His own fate has taught him that only people who are at ease can feel contempt for the misfortunes of others (12:5). Centuries later, Shakespeare's Romeo would express the same idea in these words: "He jests at scars that never felt a wound."

On the basis of his own experience, Job knows that all opposites are contained within the one God of the universe. Job tells Zophar that droughts and floods, deceived and deceiver, darkness and light, victory and defeat—everything stems from the one God (12: 15–25). Nevertheless, because Job has not yet seen God—has not yet realized the indivisibility of himself from the One in whom he lives and moves and has his being—Job's dualistic thought pattern forces him to feel that either he or God must be in the right. He is angry that his friends are willing to speak deceitfully on God's behalf (13:7–8) by insisting that Job must have deserved what has happened to him. But no matter how much Job's knowledge of his own innocence forces him to see God as his tormentor, nothing can make Job deny his dogged devotion to that tormentor: "Behold, [God] will slay me; I have no hope," Job cries; "yet I will defend my ways to [God's] face" (13:15).[20]

Although many readers have labored to find genuine progress in the arguments between Job and his friends, there really is none to be found. The friends certainly possess individual characteristics, and they become more vehement as time goes by (while Job becomes more calm), but everybody's basic outlook remains the same. The form of their arguing is dictated by the dualistic framework within which they argue. Nothing can change until the framework itself is questioned.

A UNIFIED VISION

Forced by his desperate circumstances to think more creatively than his accusers, Job returns to the idea of a unifying mediator and achieves a glimpse of hope: "Even now, behold, my witness is in heaven" (16:19). It is in this same spirit that Job utters the most famous words in the book that bears his name:

> For I know that my Redeemer lives,
> and at last [my Redeemer, my defender, my vindicator]
>   will stand upon the earth;
> and after my skin has been thus destroyed,
> then from my flesh I shall see God. (19:25–26)

Although Christians are eager to see this passage as a prophecy concerning Jesus, in the Hebrew context Job is saying that his acquittal is going to come sooner or later, either during this life or afterward. He will be permitted to present his case before God, and he *will* find the umpire or advocate who will prove him blameless.

In the face of his relentless accusers Job declares, "I shall see [God] for myself,/ and my eyes shall behold, and not another" (19: 27). This prophecy is fulfilled when Job sees God as undivided from himself and from all that exists. Job's comment can be taken in two ways. It can mean, "I myself, and nobody other than I, will see God with my own eyes." But it can also be taken to mean, "With my own eyes I will see God, who will be not another, but I myself." Not for one moment do I suggest that Job could have consciously intended the second meaning at this juncture in his experience. I think only that he has prophesied more than he could consciously have understood—as has his author.

Furthermore, Job's flash of intuition concerning a union between creature and Creator leads him to express the psychological correlative to that union:

> If you say, "How we will pursue him!"
> and, "The root of the matter is found in him";
> be afraid of the sword,
> that you may know there is a judgment. (19:28–29)

In other words, because all human beings are interconnected by their drawing on a single Source of energy, not only our pure core but also our tendency to distort is interrelated. What we see in other people tends to be a projection of what we are ourselves; and what we sow, we can expect to reap. Again, there is more to this statement than Job could fully have understood before seeing God: those who judge and hound other people are viewing those others as separate from themselves, and thus are denying the human indivisibility that stems from our common dependence upon God's Spirit.

Self-righteous judgmentalism brings upon the "separated" ego exactly the judgment it has meted out upon the other person. Jesus said something similar: "Judge not, that you be not judged. For with the judgment you pronounce you will be judged, and the measure you give will be the measure you get" (Matt. 7:1–2). The idea here is not to be mindless or to lack the ability to evaluate, but rather to apply to others no judgment that one has not first thoroughly applied to oneself. Because of the spiritual web joining all creatures, all thoughts (negative or positive) inevitably return to the one who generates them.

Job himself beautifully embodies his own insight that what we give is what we get. For instance, after God has dismissed Elihu with the question, "Who is this that darkens counsel/ by words without knowledge?" Job does not crow over Elihu's humiliation. Instead, Job applies to his own condition what God has said about Elihu; quoting the question, Job applies it to himself: "I have uttered what I did not understand,/ things too wonderful for me, which I did not know" (42:3). Most readers have been misled by Job's statement to assume that God had indeed rebuked Job rather than Elihu. But Job was not only telling the truth about his former delusion of separateness; he was also graciously identifying with Elihu in his shame. Having seen God, Job knows better than to gloat about another person's disgrace; for within the one creation energized by one God, we are all one. By graciously identifying with disgraced Elihu in the presence of God, Job becomes for Elihu the very mediator or umpire he had earlier desired for himself.

Similarly, in the Epilogue the three original friends are instructed to ask Job to intercede on their behalf. In this way they are forced to recognize their own self-righteous folly and Job's truthfulness, for God says, "you have not spoken of me what is right, as my servant Job has" (42:8). Notice that although Job has recently grasped a wholistic understanding of who God is (a perspective that has caused him to repent of his dualistically defined self-understanding of separateness from God), nevertheless God states that Job has been telling the truth about God all along, whereas those who sought to defend God at Job's expense were both foolish and false. Apparently God is willing to settle for human honesty about human experience! Job was true to his own firsthand experience, however limited it may have been, but his friends retreated behind the security of abstract theories. Pretending to defend God, they were actually defending their own concepts, orthodoxies, and categories. Pretending to be men of faith, they acted out of fear. Now that they have to humble themselves before the man they have accused, they can feel what it is like to be needy and in the wrong. Presumably, they will never be quite the same again.

But Job does not gloat at their humiliation. Instead, as he did for Elihu, he becomes for them the umpire or advocate he had desired for himself. Touching God with one hand and his friends with the other, Job heals not only their condition but also his own. The healing and forgiveness Job gives to his friends, he gives to himself, for we are told, "And [God] restored the fortunes of Job, when he had prayed for his friends" (42:10). Job's healed perception is symbolized by the double restoration of Job's wealth, and by his fathering a second family as large as the first.

THE SIGNIFICANCE OF THE EPILOGUE

Many critics regard the Epilogue as an embarrassment because it seems to support the very doctrine Job has refuted, that serving God faithfully brings material blessings. Samuel Sandmel, for instance, faults the Epilogue for its sentimentality and lack of insight.[21] To T. R. Henn, it is simply "extrinsic."[22] But, reminding ourselves that the whole story is stylized and symbolic, we are able to view the restoration of Job's fortunes and family as symbols of the healing that takes place through at-one-ment with God, the world, and all the creatures in it.

Furthermore, the Job of the Epilogue really is a changed man. He is open to the comfort and consolation of his friends concerning the devastating experience he has lived through (42:11). Having identified with the God of darkness as well as light, Job is free to acknowledge his own dark places, his depressions. And whereas none of Job's seven sons and three daughters had been named in the Prologue, and the second set of sons remains nameless in the Epilogue, the three daughters are named there (42:14)—a surprising detail in the literature of a patriarchal culture. We are also told that, in contrast to custom, Job granted an inheritance to his daughters along with their brothers (42:15). Apparently Job's own experience of being powerless had increased his sensitivity to the powerlessness of others in society! Daughters in a wealthy household like Job's would have been victims of a sexist oppression that was an almost invisible part of the accepted power structure. Thus, Job's first set of daughters had always been invited to the feasts their brothers gave; but the sons had their own houses, while the daughters did not (1:4). It's one thing to be invited to someone else's house for a party; it is something else to own one's own house and be able to give one's own parties! When Job's power is restored, he combines a new awareness with his already strong sense of justice. Like the redeemed King Lear, Job takes special care of those whom society has traditionally disinherited.

These details are intimately involved in Job's repentance, for a wholistic vision of God's nature calls into being a wholistic response to the creation. When Job was acting only according to what his ears had heard concerning the Holy One, he thought of God as a very tidy being who needed to be placated for any possible deviation from positive and grateful attitudes. So totally had he trained himself in praise that when he hears of the loss of his wealth, servants, and children by various catastrophies, his first reaction is to worship (1:20). Part of Job's blamelessness is that he is able to be objectively fair even about his own fate: having taken so many gifts from the Almighty, he comments, he must be willing also to accept deprivation of those gifts.

Or so Job's theory goes. We see things differently after Job and his friends have sat in grieved silence together for an entire week (2:12). (Incidentally, we must not be too quick to condemn Job's friends until we have sat with our own friends nonjudgmentally and sympathetically for a solid week when their fortunes are worse than our own!) Only after the week of silence does Job reveal that he had placated God with sacrifices for himself and his children, having done so out of fear of exactly the kind of ruin that has occurred: "For the thing that I fear comes upon me,/ and what I dread befalls me" (3:25). And it is not long before Job discovers the one deprivation he cannot endure: being deprived of the respect and honor he has always enjoyed as a wealthy and powerful man. It is the accusation of his friends, based on their dualistic concept that suffering must be the fault either of God or the sufferer, that drives Job from praising God to desiring courtroom justice.

Yet the change is not as great as it might seem at first; for whether Job was placating and praising God in his prosperity or raging at God and pleading for a mediator in his misery, Job's understanding of God's nature was as dualistic as that of his friends. Job's greatness lies in his refusal to capitulate to the pressure of their easy answers. He refuses to lie about himself—and, as it turns out, truth about his own experience is truth about God also (even if distorted by dualistic categories). Surely a major point of the Book of Job is that we are well advised to speak only on the basis or our own firsthand experience, sticking strictly to what we know by living it. Although our God may be much too *small*, at least we will be relating to reality instead of to our own dogmatic, prefabricated, comfortable delusions!

The God who is revealed in the whirlwind is anything but comfortable. This is the God of both the morning stars and the gates of death, the God of tempests and the lovely Pleiades, the God of wild donkeys and oxen who will not help human beings with their work, the God of lions and raven and their prey, the God of the swift ostrich who lacks maternal instinct, the Creator of the monstrous behemoth, the Creator who can also destroy creation at will (40: 19), and, above all, the God of the dread leviathan who "makes the deep boil like a pot" (41:31). This God is both father to the rain and dew and mother to the ice and frost (38:28–29). For this untidy, all-encompassing God is beyond human sexual limitations and beyond human judgments concerning good and evil. Seeing this God, Job gasps, "I know that thou canst do all things,/ and that no purpose of thine can be thwarted" (42:2).

Seeing this God, Job grasps that questions about his own righteousness are inconsequential because, after all, he is caught up in the workings of a God who is the process and the structure of everything that is real. Of any smaller, more fragmented view, Job repents. D. D. Raphael charges that the Book of Job lacks tragic stature because "the grandeur of the hero is deliberately shrunk to nothing before the sublimity of the power he has questioned."[23] And so it seems, *if* one is looking at Job and God through dualistic lenses. But if Job realizes a fusion with the sublime power that cannot be packaged, controlled, or explained, he becomes simultaneously nothing *and everything*. He does not in fact lose his heroic proportions; rather, his adventure is converted from tragedy to divine comedy.

THE TRANSFORMATION OF JOB

Because of Job's repentance—because of his new and larger, humbling and exhilarating identification with the One God—Job is able to permit himself greater joy and greater sorrow than he had acknowledged prior to his tribulations. He no longer denies his negative feelings, for he allows his friends to comfort him when he is down; and he is able to enjoy the company of his children. Before his trials, Job's sons had held feasts in their own homes; apparently Job's role had been limited to worrying about the possibility of their angering God (1:4–5). But after he sees God in the whirlwind and repents, the family feasts are in Job's own house (42:11). From this detail we may perhaps conclude that Job's new sense of oneness with the universal process has made him considerably easier to live with.

We might even go as far as poet Archibald MacLeish when in commenting on the relationship between his drama *J.B.* and the Book of Job. MacLeish says that in the Job Epilogue

> love becomes the ultimate human answer to the ultimate human question. Love, in reason's terms, answers nothing. . . . [But] what love does is affirm. It affirms the worth of life in spite of life. . . . J.B., like Job, covers his mouth with his hand, acquiesces in the vast indifference of the universe as all must who truly face it: takes his life back again. In love. To live.[24]

But it is my contention that the universe (and God) look *indifferent* only to those whose deluded egos separate them from the One Who Is. Although I reject MacLeish's perception of indifference, I agree that Job's Epilogue implies that the process of living in love is the process that confers meaning upon the vast, unexplained mysteries of human experience. Living in love (which involves doing justice) is godding.

A Presbyterian preacher named Thomas John Carlisle has summarized the meaning of Job's repentance in a poem entitled "Whirlwind Courtship":

> With what dark humor
> God engages
> [God's] quarry
> offering counsel
> with blockbusters
> and thunderbolts
> of naturalistic knowledge
> watching and waiting
> for the sudden turn
> the converting moment
> when [God's] beloved target
> will center and understand
> that One who works in wonders
> works in him.[25]

The Book of Job depicts a person who was morally blameless from the beginning and who refused to violate his integrity by assuming false blame for the sake of preserving orthodox doctrines. After seeing for himself the all-encompassing nature of the God who made and empowers both lamb and tiger, Job repents of the smaller vision that had separated his own perfection and pain from the larger context of the perfection and pain of God—lions, frosts, leviathan, and all. Job realizes that the same One who works those wonders is also at work within the wonders of his everyday life. If there is no rational justification for Job's suffering, no conceptual response to his desire for vindication, that is as it should be. Job sees that the God of the universe is "selving God's Self" through Job's life, through both easy and difficult experiences. And that is enough for Job.

WHAT ABOUT US ORDINARY PEOPLE?

It takes enormous courage to "god" in the way that Job "godded." Whenever I read the Book of Job, I am overwhelmed by Job's courage, by his refusal to be browbeaten into lying about himself in order to preserve God's good name. I think about my own nervous inner waffling, the terror I feel when I must assert (against voices in my environment) that, yes, my experience really *is* God's working within me and not merely my own sin, or heresy, or egotism. Did Job feel no temptation to betray his own truth in order to keep peace? I wonder. In fact, it might be possible to become discouraged by Job's example, because the rest of us could never measure up. Job was, after all, a legendary hero, not any ordinary person!

But I choose instead to be empowered by Job's transformation from dogged, joyless, but faithful godding when he thought the Holy One was totally other from himself, to joyous and sensitive godding after he has seen his identity with the One who is simultaneously within him yet far greater than he. The point is not that I must be as great as Job; the point is that I must be *myself*, so that God can achieve embodiment within me, as God did in Job. If I deny my own experience and speak what I think is *supposed to be true* rather than what my experience has taught me, then my attempts at godding will be inauthentic, mere noisy gongs and clanging cymbals. But if I stick to what life has taught me, no matter how far short I fall of the *whole* truth about God, at least my limited vision will be real and open to further revelations.

Certainly when we human beings move beyond dualistic categories which place God across a great unbridgeable chasm as the Totally Other with whom we have nothing in common—when we see instead that the "One who works in wonders/works in *us*"—then, like the repenting Job, we are empowered to enjoy life and to share our joy and power with those who have less than we. We are encouraged toward a godding filled both with laughter and with the social awareness that does justice to those people who were formerly excluded from the good basics of life.

NOTES

1. Robert Alter, *The Art of Biblical Narrative* (New York: Basic Books, 1981), p. 33. Moses Maimonides called the Book of Job an allegory; see Jack Kahn, *Job's Illness: Loss, Grief, and Integration* (New York: Pergamon Press, 1975), p. 153. And cf. Samuel Sandmel: "Even in the days of the ancient rabbis [Job] was recognized as a work of creativity, not as a record of a historical man. The poet has illuminated the experience of men [and women] through a poem about a man" (*The Enjoyment of Scripture* (New York: Oxford, 1972), p. 236). Bible quotations are from *The New Oxford Annotated Bible* (RSV), 1977, sometimes modified in the direction of inclusiveness.

2. "Job," in *Asimov's Guide to the Bible: The Old Testament* (New York: Avon, 1968), p. 474.

3. *Understanding the Old Testament*, 3d ed. (Englewood Cliffs, NJ: Prentice-Hall, 1957), pp. 556–59.

4. James S. Ackerman, Alan Wilkin Jenks, Edward B. Jenkinson, Jan Blough, *Teaching the Old Testament in English Classes* (Bloomington: Indiana University Press, 1973), p. 417.

5. See T. R. Henn's interesting discussion in *The Bible as Literature* (New York: Oxford University Press, 1970), p. 160.

6. Bernhard W. Anderson, *Rediscovering the Bible* (New

York: Association Press, 1960), p. 142. Although he in no way accuses Job of sin, Carl Jung seems somewhat anti-Semitic because he treats the whole Book of Job as a prelude to the Christian doctrine of incarnation. Yahweh is forced by Job's incorruptibility to change his nature into a more conscious, more amiable one. Thus, one of the great masterpieces of the Hebrew Scripture becomes for Jung an antechamber to the Christian Scriptures. See "Answer to Job," in *The Collected Works of Carl Jung*, Vol. 11, *Psychology and Religion* (Princeton University Press, 1969), pp. 357–470.

7. *A Guide to Understanding the Bible* (New York: Harper and Row, 1938), pp. 165–67.

8. *Introduction to the Old Testament* (Nashville: Abingdon Press, 1968), p. 334.

9. "The Book of Job," in *Twentieth Century Interpretations of Job*, ed. Paul S. Sanders (Englewood Cliffs, NJ: Prentice-Hall, 1968), p. 27.

10. *The Bible as Literature: The Old Testament and the Apocrypha* (New York: Barnes and Noble, 1970), p. 286.

11. *A Literary Survey of the Bible* (Plainfield, NJ: Logos International, 1973), p. 74.

12. *Introduction to the Old Testament* (New York: Harper and Brothers, 1938), p. 707.

13. *The Literature of the Bible* (Grand Rapids, MI: Zondervan Publishing House, 1974), p. 117.

14. *Asimov's Guide to the Bible: The Old Testament* (New York: Avon Books, 1968), p. 487.

15. *The Enjoyment of Scripture* (New York: Oxford University Press, 1972), pp. 233–36.

16. Wilfrid J. Harrington, O.P., *Key to the Bible*, Vol. 2, *The Old Testament* (Garden City, NY: Doubleday Image Books, 1976), p. 124.

17. Marvin H. Pope, "Job, Book of," in *The Interpreter's Dictionary of the Bible*, Vol. 2 (Nashville: Abingdon Press, 1962), p. 920.

18. Ibid., p. 920.

19. Wright and Fuller, *The Book of the Acts of God: Contemporary Scholarship Interprets the Bible* (Garden City, NY: "Dou-

bleday-Anchor, 1960), p. 196. Eugene Goodheart, "Job and the Modern World," in *Twentieth Century Interpretations of the Book of Job*, p. 99.

20. Pope (*Job*, p. 912) explains that the Greek Septuagint is sometimes so far from the Hebrew that it constitutes a radical reinterpretation. In Job 13:15, the Septuagint translators completely revamped the verse in order to make it sound less bitter, and their practice has been reflected by most English translators, making the outcry read something like, "Though [God] slay me, yet will I trust in [God]."

21. *The Enjoyment of Scripture*, pp. 222 and 236.

22. *The Bible as Literature*, p. 144.

23. "Tragedy and Religion," in *Twentieth Century Interpretations of the Book of Job*, p. 53.

24. "About a Trespass on a Monument," *The New York Times* (Dec. 7, 1958) reprinted in Roland Bartel et al., *Biblical Images in Literature* (Nashville: Abingdon Press, 1975), pp. 377–78.

25. *Journey with Job* (Grand Rapids, MI: William B. Eerdmans, 1976), p. 85.

3

Godding toward Religious Inclusiveness

Over a century ago, the great American poet Emily Dickinson wrote a satire of timid ladies that actually satirizes timid attitudes in general. She wrote,

> What soft, cherubic creatures
> These gentlewomen are.
> One would as soon assault a plush
> Or violate a star!
>
> Such dimity convictions!
> A horror so refined
> Of freckled human nature,
> Of deity ashamed.
>
> It's such a common glory,
> A fisherman's degree—
> Redemption, brittle lady,
> Be so ashamed of thee![1]

Emily Dickinson asserts here that if one is too refined to accept human nature with all its flaws and freckles, one is actually ashamed of God's very Self—for it is through human relationships that the nature of God is humanly incarnated. To have a genuine and meaningful theology, Dickinson says, is a "common glory" not reserved for the aristocracy or the intellectual elite, but available to everyone. It is lowly, "a fisherman's degree." Although Dickinson begins by calling timid women "soft, cherubic creatures," referring to woman's nineteenth-century assigned role as "the angel in the house," by the end of the poem she has struck through the soft, cherubic mask and has found only brittleness:

> Redemption, brittle lady,
> Be so ashamed of thee!

Dimity is a very thin, sheer cotton fabric: it is impossible to keep oneself warm in dimity. Addressing the nineteenth-century Christians in her own environment, Dickinson suggests that when our convictions are "dimity" and when we are so refined that we shrink from "freckled human nature," we are actually ashamed of deity—and in return, Redemption is ashamed of us. Dickinson uses the word redemption here in the figure of speech known as metonymy; that is, she takes just one trait associated by Christians with Jesus of Nazareth and allows that trait to stand for the Christ's whole nature. What she is telling us is that if our theology is not big enough to encompass the complexities of human nature and all the variety within creation as we find it, then we are ashamed of the Creator and Redeemer, and in response the Creator and Redeemer is ashamed of us. By contrast, Jesus tells us about the surprising traits of those who move with nature and the God of nature, rather than opposing the natural creation. Jesus said:

> The wind blows wherever it pleases. You hear its sound, but you cannot tell where it comes from or where it is going. So it is with everyone [who is] born of the Spirit. (John 3:8, NIV).

A THEOLOGY OF THE WIND

Because I am a Christian and because I think my own family of faith needs to learn inclusiveness perhaps more than any other, I must now utilize specifically Christian terminology. It is my conviction that godding, a conscious cooperation infused with the Holy Spirit, calls us toward an all-inclusive attitude, a theology of the wind, a relationship to God and the world that does not try to make things easy by ruling out whole areas of human experience and whole groups of human beings. A person who fishes must deal with whatever turns up in the fish net. When one goes out to fish, one does not dictate to God what may or may not be attracted to the bait. One may plead, but one may not dictate! Similarly, I find that godding calls people toward a lowly "common glory," a fisher's degree that lays aside its "dimity convictions" and learns that *nothing human is alien to a viable theology.*

Many churches have built a theology that works beautifully, but only for the people in power: the relatively wealthy, predominantly white, predominantly male, predominantly middle-aged, fully abled, self-consciously heterosexual married membership. Thousands of people are excluded by such a theology and the unconscious assumptions fostered by it. The fact that churches do not *consciously intend* to exclude anyone is no excuse. Instead of bemoaning the fact that some women and other minority people have begun to clamor for first-class citizenship, church members may rejoice that we are being offered the opportunity to move toward wholeness —not just the wholeness of Christ's body, the church, but also our own internal wholeness. Let me explain what I mean by that.

INCLUSIVENESS AFFECTS PERSONAL AND INSTITUTIONAL WHOLENESS

When we possess any measure of power, we human beings have a persistent tendency to divide other people into categories of "us" and "them." Inevitably, we define *us* as having the traits we consider positive and acceptable and admirable. We define *them* as having the traits we do not want to admit that we ourselves may possess. For centuries the white race has done this to people of darker colors: *we*, the whites, are responsible and caring; *they*, the dark-skinned people, are irresponsible and shiftless, and therefore must be controlled by us. Men have done the same thing to women: *we*, the men, are logical and unafraid; *they*, the women, are childish and full of irrational fear. One current example of this in the church is what is being done to gay and lesbian Christians who seek ordination, or first-class citizenship in the church. The heterosexual majority—*we*—has defined itself as sexually responsible and full of spiritual concern; but the gay and lesbian Christians—*they*—are lustful, irresponsibly promiscuous, and without God in their minds.

The process of splitting us from them is so persistent and reasserts itself with such dogged determination that I have come to regard it as the essence of sin. And I predict that if and when any church develops a truly inclusive theology that steadfastly rejects us-versus-them categories, there will be an influx of relief and well-being among all those who can open themselves to that theology.

To bring home to the heart of the church all those we have defined as the "other" is to give ourselves permission to acknowledge and accept within ourselves those traits we have been denying. White people will be able to acknowledge their own irresponsibilities and will not have to project them onto darker-skinned people; men will be free to acknowledge their own irrational fears and childishness and will not be forced to project them onto women; heterosexuals will be free to acknowledge their own lustful urges and will no longer have to project them onto homosexuals and bisexuals. And so forth. The reward for an inclusive theology is enormous! It is nothing less than a restoration to *wholeness* of the body of Christ, and a granting of permission to each individual member of Christ's body to accept *all* aspects of themselves and thus to move toward wholeness.

US-VERSUS-THEM ATTITUDES: BOTH DELUSORY AND SINFUL

A paragraph ago I said that I have come to regard the us-versus-them categorizing tendency as the very essence of sin. I'd like to document that by reference to what the apostle Paul said to the Athenian philosophers on Mars Hill, as recorded in Acts 17. Paul explained to them that

[God] is not served by human hands, as if [God] needed anything, because [God, God's very Self] gives to all [human beings] life and breath and everything else. From one [person, God] made every nation of [humankind], that they should inhabit the whole earth . . . . God did this so that [human beings] would seek [God] and perhaps reach out for [God] and find [God], though [God] is not far from each one of us. "For in [God] we live and move and have our being." As some of your own poets have said, "We are [God's] offspring" (NIV, inclusive language mine).

In this well-known passage Saint Paul insists that God's reason for creating so much variety in the human race—so many nations over the whole earth—is precisely so that human beings would seek and find God, in whose tremendous womb all of us live and move and have our being. If we are the offspring of one heavenly Parent who is not only our Father but also our Mother, then to attack another human being is to attack a sister or brother. But more: if every human being lives and moves and has being *within God's being,* as Paul asserts, then to draw circles that exclude other people is to create a civil war within the all-encompassing nature of God. By rejecting or excluding others, we cut ourselves off from the experience of God's love for our own entire being—the shadowy "them" characteristics as well as the sunlit "us" characteristics.

In a nuclear world, us-versus-Them categories are too dangerous an indulgence. For as R. D. Laing has said, "We are Them to Them as they are Them to us." And in the process of wiping out them, we will wipe out us as well. But we don't need a nuclear holocaust to teach us that lesson; we can see it in our own psychological experience, any time we take the time to look. What we give to other people is what we give to ourselves. As Jesus told us, the judgment we mete out is the same judgment we ourselves will be judged by.

The implication of Scripture seems to be that we find God *in the otherness of the other.* We find God precisely when we drop our us-versus-them categories and open ourselves to that which we had previously rejected. To deny the "freckled," variegated, pluralistic nature of humanity is to be ashamed of what God created. To affirm pluralism is to affirm the Creator. If we take seriously the things Saint Paul said on Mars Hill, human oneness is a fact because the oneness of God's all-encompassing nature is a fact, and all of us live and move and have our being within God. If that's a fact, then to live according to us-versus-them categories is a delusion as well as a sin. To affirm the diversity of the human race while at the same time affirming our unity in one God is to come home to reality.

To speak more concretely about inclusiveness, let's consider now some of the areas where it seems most difficult for Christian people in the United States to give up the sin and delusion of us-versus-them separateness.

YIELDING UP NATIONALISM

As Christians in the United States of America, we first must give up our dream of being the number-one nation in the world and must move toward international cooperation in stewardship of the oceans, the atmosphere, and an environment conducive to the good health of the human race. Ten years ago the politically conservative Committee on the Present Danger—including Ronald Reagan, Jeane Kirkpatrick, and others—stated that "the principal threat to our nation, to world peace, and to the cause of human freedom is *the Soviet drive for dominance* based upon an unparalleled military buildup."[2] This amounts, of course, to saying that our greatest danger is *them.* Despite changes in Soviet leadership since 1976, President Reagan has never wavered from this 1976 perception, which explains, for instance, his opposition to the Sandinista government in Nicaragua, his behavior toward Qaddafi, and his defiance of nuclear test ban agreements.

In 1976 the Committee on the Present Danger expressed the fear that the United States would become "second best to the Soviet Union in overall military strength," after which "we could find ourselves isolated in a hostile world." They warned that "our national survival itself would be in peril." I find it ironic that out of fear of losing our separate nationhood, the United States has earned the reputation of being the most *violent* nation in the world, the only nation to have used nuclear weapons on other people, the nation that is proposing to put armaments even into space, the nation that refuses to renounce the first use of nuclear weapons, as China and the Soviet Union have done. If it is isolation we fear, what could be more isolating than our own national egotism and military muscle flexing?

The world's economies are interdependent. Problems of

diminished energy resources, inadequate health care, environmental pollution, hunger, radioactive wastes, and the like, do no stop at national borders. As for national survival, what would it profit any individual nation to survive in a nuclear wasteland? The world community is fragile, vulnerable, and complex. We must direct our willpower and our energy in the direction of enhancing the security of the whole world by active peacekeeping measures.

Peace has been defined in a positive fashion as the opposite not merely of war, but of all violence, including structural violence. Peace is thus the opposite of whatever inhibits the growth and fulfillment of any human being. In other words, a positive peace requires the active presence of justice for all.

Gandhi defined peace as a state in which every person is fully realized. Saint Augustine defined it as the ordered tranquility of all parts of a system. Michael Nagler defined peace as "that state in which all parties spontaneously desire one another's welfare."[3] All of this sounds a great deal like the concept of mutuality in the Christian Scriptures: "Be subject to one another out of reverence for Christ" (Eph. 6:21, RSV).

Positive peace making has very little to do with negative definitions of peace as the absence of organized physical conflict. According to that negative definition, a huge missile, an instrument of brutal mass destruction, has been christened the Peacekeeper. What an irony!

In contrast to "keeping peace" by threatening destruction, people who are committed to godding will love the world as God loves it and will work for the survival of the earth and all the people on it. They will not stop at working toward a halt of the testing, production, and deployment of nuclear weapons. They will work also at strengthening the instruments of a positive peace, such as appropriate economic development that would provide jobs for unemployed people around the world.

If we truly believe that all human beings are the children

of one divine Parent, we will put our money, time, and energy where our mouths are. In particular, women must teach their sons, husbands, brothers, and male friends that it takes more courage to connect than it does to destroy. Patriarchal society has defined courage in terms of its destructive power. I remember that my college History of Civilization course was organized entirely around wars and conquests. Men were great in proportion to their courage to destroy. But the Bible teaches a different kind of courage, the courage to speak truthfully and lovingly and to listen carefully—the courage to connect. As opposed to the instrumentality of male socialization, female socialization has stressed relationship; hence, it is mainly up to women to teach a new and peacemaking form of courage to the men in our lives. Do we have the courage to give up our "dimity convictions" in order to take on the "common glory" of global concern?

YIELDING UP DENOMINATIONALISM

If indeed the Body of Christ or the world Christian community is to become an active peacekeeping community, we Christians will also have to yield up our us-versus-them delusions when it comes to denominationalism. This does not mean that Catholics and Protestants, Lutherans and Presbyterians, Methodists and Baptists, and all the other denominations will be forced to hammer out a set of doctrines and a set of liturgies on which everyone can agree. (I'd hate to hold my breath waiting for that one!) Rather, we should return to the model set forth by Saint Paul on Mars Hill: from one source God has made the human race enormously varied and diverse, and all of that variation and diversity is accurately recognized as coming from one divine parentage. In God all of us "live and move and have our being." From one, many;

though many, one. The goal of ecumenism is not a syncretistic enforcement of a single way of doing things, but rather the sharing of a faith-experience that is far more profound than any denominational difference.

The goal of ecumenism is not dogmatic, doctrinal, or even liturgical agreement. The goal of ecumenism is mutual cooperation and respect as the affirmation of a single faith-experience, a shared membership in the New Creation. According to Saint Paul, this New Creation is a just and fair world in which the barriers of racism, classism, and sexism are melted, in which there is no longer any them but only a global us:

> for as many of you as were baptised into Christ have put on Christ. There is neither Jew nor Greek, there is neither slave nor free, there is neither male nor female, for you are all one in Christ Jesus. (Gal. 3:27–28, RSV)

YIELDING UP CHRISTIANITY'S EXCLUSIVE CLAIMS

Harder for most of us to understand and accept is that not only must we Christians yield up our denominational territorialism; we must also yield up our Christian territorialism! By that I mean that if we Christians want an inclusive church, we must move toward genuine interreligious dialogue and cooperation, consciously ridding ourselves of our triumphalist Christology and our unconscious anti-Semitism. If our vision of a New Creation in Christ Jesus includes only those people who have made a conscious commitment to the Christian religion, "what about all those women and men in the world who have been damaged, or done in, by the Christian claim to be a special place in the world of God?" As the Reverend Dr. Carter Heyward has written:

> Any Christology which is proclaimed uncritically—whether simply out of habit or out of ecclesial anxiety about what it

may mean for the church to let go of its triumphalist Christ—sets up barriers to the possibility of any real solidarity with most people in the world.[4]

I think Dr. Heyward is right about that. And rather than shrugging our shoulders about it, and claiming that we are simply bearing "the offense of the cross" in our exclusivism, I think we Christians might profit by learning to worship God more as Jesus himself worshiped God. It was Jesus who told us the story of a tax collector who went up to the temple to pray but was so ashamed of his sin that he simply cried out for God's mercy—and went home justified! If Jesus himself told us about God's salvation given to someone who had never heard of (let alone believed in) "the cross-work of Christ," how dare we assume that justification as we Christians define it is the *only* justification there is? As Jesus said in his identity as the Good Shepherd, "I have other sheep, that are not of this fold" (John 10:16, RSV).

Instead of bearing these teachings in mind and thus following the religion *of* Jesus, Christians have developed a religion *about* Jesus. Everything Jesus is known to have said and done on earth fits into the model of a renewal movement within Judaism, the laws of which Jesus said he came "not to destroy, but to fulfill." But instead of seeing Jesus as renewing, fulfilling, and deepening Judaism, many of us have assumed that Christianity is the successor to Judaism and, properly understood, serves to wipe out the Jewish presence by subsuming Jews into Christianity or else condemning them to hell. The fact that the Nazis could destroy so many Jewish lives in our own century with so little protest from Christians proves that we need to do some hard and self-conscious work on the attitudes embedded in Christian theology.

When Jesus says, "Nobody comes to the Father [and Mother] but by me," might he not be referring to an abiding sense of oneness with his divine Source, a sense of organic union

that Jesus never forgot? No one comes to God except by remembering that organic oneness with the Source of us all!
And when Saint Paul speaks of being "in Christ," isn't he referring to the new, inclusive, love- and justice-oriented attitudes of the New Humanity in the New Creation? Given his
personal experiences, and his role as the Apostle to the Gen-
tiles, Paul of course used specifically Christian terminology
for the beautiful and liberating concept that to be "in Christ"
means the end of exclusions based on race, class, and sex.
Twentieth-century Christians need not apologize for the
high value we place on Christian terminology concerning the
New Humanity. My point is *not* that we must surrender our
Christian terminology. Rather, when we use it we must
learn to make clear that although we use Christian terms out
of our own life experience, we understand that other religions may have their own terms for similar visions. Our primary interest is not in insisting on our own terms, but rather
in bringing about the New Creation purged of racism, sexism, and classism. Our common goal is the New Humanity in
the New Creation. Much as our hearts may throb with joy to
affirm the sovereignty of Jesus the Christ, our task of creating
a just and decent society requires that we learn to speak and
think more inclusively than we have done.

This change in perspective I have described has been important in my own experience. I was brought up in American
fundamentalism, got my undergraduate degree from Bob
Jones University, and remained a fundamentalist well into
my thirties. I still remember the shock I received when I first
read the fourteenth-century mystical treatise *The Cloud of
Unknowing*. Its thesis is that the facts we think we know
about God must be laid aside if we are ever to have a direct
experience *of* God. Now, fundamentalism is a very rational-
istic form of Christianity; I was taught the answers to questions long before I knew that there *were* questions. So for me
it was a terrible blow to hear that if I were to meet God, I

would have to give up my armor of doctrines and enter into a cloud of *unknowing!*

I think that the Christian community as a whole, even the nonfundamentalists among us, would be blessed by remembering that everything we say about God is only metaphoric and never the literal truth. Although the Bible gives us a multitude of images concerning God as our Father, Mother, Friend, and various natural phenomena such as Wind, Rock, and Water, we would do well to remember that even these are only images, only the language of accommodation that tempers the huge winds of reality to the shorn lambskins of our mortal understandings. I have argued elsewhere that using the full range of biblical imagery for God will force our minds to remember that God is literally none of these and therefore will free us from the idolatry that has grown up around the single image of God as Father.[5] My point here is that by entering often into the cloud of unknowing, by reminding ourselves often that God is far beyond anything we can say about God, we Christians may develop a more wholesome respect for the approaches taken by other religions and thus become a more inclusive church. The question once again is this: Do we Christians have the courage to give up our "dimity convictions" and embrace a "common glory?"

INCLUSIVENESS IN LOCAL CONGREGATIONS

We have discussed international inclusiveness and interdenominational and interreligious inclusiveness. Now I would like to discuss inclusiveness within the local congregation. It is not enough to put out a sign saying "Everybody is welcome." It is also not enough to specifically invite people of other colors, or disabled people, or gay and lesbian people to join the congregation. To invite a single, divorced, or gay person to our church and then speak and act as if everybody in the world were heterosexually married is the equivalent of inviting a hearing-impaired person to our church and then failing to provide an interpreter for the hearing impaired! We are only providing opportunity for people to feel deliberately excluded.

It is *not* inclusive merely to invite minority people to hear majority or normative viewpoints from the pulpit. An inclusive congregation will recognize the different voices of the various nonnormative groups, and will carefully provide opportunity for their various views to be heard as important influences in congregational decisions.

Women have been part of Christian congregations for centuries, but Christian congregations have not been inclusive of women insofar as the insights of women have not been sought and the leadership of women has not been fully utilized. Most churches to this day are not really inclusive of women. When we see women serving at every level of decision making and leadership in the exact proportion that there are women sitting in the pews, then we will know that we are looking at a congregation that is inclusive of women. When we see a national church in which the percentage of women bishops, pastors, and lay leaders corresponds to the percentage of women in the pews, then we will know we are looking at a national church that is inclusive of women. And the same is true of gay and lesbian people: this group has a great deal to offer the church, a spirituality that has been honed by some very special pressures. The same is true of people with physical handicaps, people whose limitations have perhaps caused them to develop some very special gifts. And a congregation that has only one skin color is truly disadvantaged!

When I began to speak and write as a Christian feminist (an advocate of human equality and mutuality), I thought it was enough merely to lift up the biblical imagery of human oneness. I got a rude shock when a black Christian feminist told a group of us white Christian feminists that we ought to get our feet off her neck! She explained that unless white feminists learned to listen carefully to the specific agenda of black feminists, and helped to bring about the changes *they* were yearning for, then any white-feminist talk about unity was just more of the arrogance that says, "We are one and both of us are me." How many marriages have been built on that model, with the husband utterly sincere in his feelings of unity with his wife, utterly unaware that his fulfillment is the only fulfillment that has ever mattered in the relationship? His unconscious message to her is "We are one and both of us are me!" (I will certainly concede that there have been marriages in which the wife has done that to her husband, but such relationships are not sanctioned by society and hence are less frequent).

My point here is that an inclusive church must not simply emphasize *unity*, but must respect and revere the *diversity* that will make up the harmony of the whole. We must *listen to the various voices* of the groups that are not white, not male, not heterosexual, not fully abled, not wealthy. We must *seek to implement policies* that are fair to such people. We must *seek representation* for them in all decision-making bodies of our church. And we must use language that recognizes their presence.

USING INCLUSIVE LANGUAGE

One way to avoid excluding many people in the average congregation would be to speak of a relationship or partnership rather than exclusively using the word marriage. And it is important to realize that to speak of the Christ always as he is to deny the Christedness of women, the presence and contribution of women within the Body of Christ.

The bad habit of referring to Christ exclusively as "he" comes from unconsciously using the word Christ as the surname of Jesus, who was a human male. According to traditional Christology, in the incarnation God took on human limitations, which would include the limitation of having to be one sex or the other. Since Jesus attempted to teach us that the proper use of power was to serve those who have less power than ourselves, it seems obvious that Jesus would of necessity have to be in the power group, the free male group. But after the Resurrection and the Ascension, Jesus is the transcendent and all inclusive Christ, "the firstborn of many [sisters and] brothers" (Rom. 8:29). So we need to watch our pronouns!

As a member of the National Council of Churches' Inclusive Language Lectionary Committee, I could go on and on about the importance of the language we use. The unconscious mind is exceedingly literal, and the messages we send to it by the imagery we use concerning God are taken very literally. Nobody can speak of God as "He" and get anything but a literally male image in the unconscious mind.

I can recall from my own experience a good example of the literalness of the unconscious mind and its power over our behavior. When I was young, I showed one of my drawings to my elder brother, who was and is an excellent artist. He sucked in his breath with disgust, hissing the advice I never forgot: "Virginia, *stick to words!*" It was forty years later that I realized that my unconscious mind had programmed me so literally that not only had I feared drawing, but also mathematics, nonverbal reasoning, scientific experimentation, and even interior decorating and gardening!

Church people who think there is no problem in referring to God exclusively as "He"—and there are many such people— need to allow for the possibility that they are in a holding pattern dictated by their unconscious minds. Scripture contains so many different images of God that the problem Christians have with inclusive God-language certainly does not stem from the Bible. In fact, to follow the usage of Scripture by using many different images of God along with the pronouns relevant to each image would be the best way to clear our minds of their unconscious idolatry, their unconscious assumption that God is *literally* Father. The introduction and appendix of *An Inclusive Language Lectionary* can be helpful to anyone desiring further instruction in linguistic inclusiveness.[6]

It may *sound* very loving, very soft and cherubic, to say, "We are all one in Christ." But if our language, attitudes, and church structures exclude everyone who does not look, act, and think precisely as we do, then our *real* message is, "We are one and all of us are me." And underneath the soft cherubic mask lies the real truth: a brittleness that refuses to grow and change and modify in response to the changing direction of the wind of God's Spirit. Across the centuries the word of Jesus comes to us:

> The wind blows wherever it pleases. You hear its sound, but you cannot tell where it comes from or where it is going. So it is with everyone [who is] born of the Spirit. (John 3:8, NIV)

Do we have the courage to "god," to act like people who are born of the Spirit? Do we have the courage to live in the wind? Do we have the courage to lay aside our thin little "dimity convictions" and assume instead the lowly "*common glory*?" For the sake of the whole human race and the God who made and loves and energizes us all, I pray we do.

NOTES

1. *The Norton Anthology of Literature by Women*, ed. Sandra Gilbert and Susan Gubar (New York: W. W. Norton, 1985), p. 849. Punctuation mine.

2. "Common Sense and Common Danger," in *The Nuclear Predicament: A Sourcebook*, ed. Donna Athus Gregory (New York: St. Martin's Press, 1986), p. 205. Emphasis mine.

3. "Redefining Peace," in *The Nuclear Predicament*, pp. 331–32.

4. "An Unfinished Symphony of Liberation: The Radicalization of Christian Feminism Among White U.S. Women," *Journal of Feminist Studies in Religion*, vol. 2, no. 1 (Spring 1985), p. 116.

5. See Virginia Ramey Mollenkott, *The Divine Feminine: Biblical Imagery of God as Female* (New York: Crossroad, 1983).

6. *An Inclusive Language Lectionary: Readings for Year A, Year B, and Year C* (3 volumes) is published by John Knox Press (Atlanta), Pilgrim Press (New York), and Westminster Press (Philadelphia). Also helpful is *Language and the Church: Articles and Designs for Workshops*, ed. Barbara A. Withers (available for $10.00 from Room 704, 475 Riverside Drive, New York, N.Y. 10115-0050).

4

Godding in the Dark

Several times I have asked audiences to use a technique called clustering, introduced by Gabrielle Rico in her book *Writing the Natural Way.* I have asked people to cluster ideas around the word that is the focus of this chapter: darkness. Perhaps readers would like to try clustering for themselves before reading any farther. The idea is to draw a circle in the center of a piece of blank paper, leaving plenty of room around it for other circles to nestle, or cluster. The circles should be contiguous, not concentric. In the center circle one should write the focus word, phrase, or idea—in this case, darkness. Whatever associations pop into one's mind should be written, unedited, in the other circles nestling around the central circle.[1]

When I have asked people to do this and then to call out their association, most of the associations turn out to be negative. A few are neutral, a few are positive; but most are negative. Here is a sample cluster:

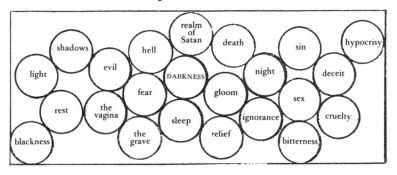

SOURCES OF NEGATIVE ATTITUDES
TOWARD DARKNESS

Western people come honestly by their negative attitudes toward darkness. Images in traditional myths, art, and Christian theology have tended to depict light as good, dark as evil. And it is a very small step from there to the idea that white is good and black is evil.

For instance, here is a poem by America's first black woman poet, Phyllis Wheatley. The poem was published in 1773 by the author's owner, a Boston tailor named John Wheatley. (Like wives today, slaves in America took the surname of their owner). The title is "On Being Brought from Africa to America":

> 'Twas mercy brought me from my pagan land,
> Taught my benighted soul to understand
> That there's a God, that there's a Saviour too:
> Once I redemption neither sought nor knew.
> Some view that sable race with scornful eye:
> "Their color is a diabolic dye."
> Remember, Christians, Negroes black as Cain
> May be refined and join the angelic strain.[2]

Of course, what Wheatley is doing here is reflecting the imagery she had been taught by her white master, and pleading for white Christians to remember that even "Negroes black as Cain," even the "sable race" with "benighted souls" who are dyed the "diabolic color" of black, may be redeemed and therefore merit some kind of human respect. Notice that in her final line Wheatley uses the image of refining or sifting Negroes until they are qualified to join the "angelic strain," the presumably white and highly spiritual race of heavenly beings. The word *refining* indicates that the Christianity Wheatley has been taught associates *blackness* with gross materiality and corporeality that must be purified before it is acceptable to God. Like women, people who are not white have been relegated to the status of *matter that must be controlled, disciplined, and refined* in order to be acceptable to God.

NEEDED: A POSITIVE THEOLOGY OF DARKNESS

This negative concept of materiality goes all the way back to the Pythagorean philosophers of ancient Greece, who taught that maleness and goodness belong to the light, but femaleness and badness belong to the dark. One Pythagorean, Empedocles, taught that sexual abstinence was the way to liberate oneself into the disembodied light.[3] I am suggesting that Christianity needs a new materialism, a respect for the body and for matter and for sexuality—for all that "darkness" images. This respect is perfectly biblical but has not been part of the emphasis of traditional Christian teachings. Imagery of darkness as positive will help to heal our racism as well. Again, I will focus on Christianity because I know it best. (Problems with what darkness suggests may be somewhat differently expressed in other religions, but are certainly present nonetheless.)

In her 1970 novel *The Bluest Eye*, black woman novelist Toni Morrison depicts a black boy named Cholly Breedlove watching an older black man holding above his head a watermelon, about to smash it for his family's eating pleasure. Cholly "wondered if God looked like that. No. God was a nice *white* man, with long white hair, flowing white beard, and little blue eyes that looked sad when people died and mean when they were bad." Cholly further mused:

> It must be the devil who looks like that—holding the world
> in his hands, ready to dash it to the ground and spill the red

> guts so niggers could eat the sweet, warm insides. If the devil did look like that, Cholly preferred him. He never felt *anything* thinking about God, but just the idea of the devil excited him. And now the strong, black devil was blotting out the sun and getting ready to split open the world.[4]

It is no surprise to me that Cholly cannot identify himself with or feel himself empowered by a white God. Like thousands of other women, I cannot identify with a *male* God; and black women of course face the double whammy. What empowers Cholly is *what is black*; and for lack of any better alternative, Cholly identifies with the devil. After much further dehumanization by white people, the adult Cholly Breedlove rapes his daughter and abandons his family.

If any reader thinks that Christian theology has recently cleaned up its act, so that our images of darkness no longer contribute to our unconscious racism and sexism and to our accompanying alienation from aspects of ourselves, look at this entry from the *Dictionary of the New Testament*, published by Harper and Row in 1980. The entry for darkness begins with the most favorable definition. Darkness is "the absence of light which typifies night. It can metaphorically describe what lies hidden." The definitions are all downhill from there. The second definition tells us that darkness is "the power over which God triumphed at the time of creation and set in order with night. An image of terror, misfortune, corruption, and death, it describes whatever is wretched." And finally, the third definition:

> Darkness is the kingdom of Satan and sin, as well as that of men who are born there in darkness [a woman's womb?] and produce wicked deeds. God is master of the darkness and snatches whomever he wills out of it into the light. Man, for his part, is caught in a combat between light and darkness (cf. Qumram), out of which the Christian emerges triumphant in his following of Christ. This victory presupposes

faith and brotherly love. As their opposite, exterior darkness
is the place of punishment located outside of heaven. (p. 156)

These definitions in *Dictionary of the New Testament*—
published, I remind you, in 1980, by a respectable publishing house—are accompanied by forty-nine supporting
biblical references. I could have demonstrated the same
thing with an article in *The Interpreter's Dictionary of the
Bible*, but that was published in 1962, and I was afraid people would think things had been corrected since then.

I do not deny that the Bible, like most of literature and art,
uses much imagery of darkness that reflects and intensifies
the human fear of darkness, both external and internal
darkness. What distresses me is that nowhere in the dictionary entry is there the slighest suggestion that darkness in
the Bible and other literature can *also* have positive,
creative, and healing significance. And from the standpoint
of human psychology, that suggestion would be nothing but
realistic.

"LIGHT" AND "DARK" THINKING

When we use the technique of clustering, we are trying to
evade the "bright" or "light" side of the brain in order to gain
access to the fertile "dark" side. Until very recently Western
education has addressed itself almost entirely to the left
brain, the lobe that controls the right, or "masculine," side of
the body, so that only the most creative people have been
able to stay in contact with the neglected right brain that
controls the left, or "feminine," or "dark" side of the body.
Even the best idea becomes harmful when upheld to the exclusion of its opposite, and education in the Western world
has stressed logic and linear thinking so exclusively that the

emphasis has turned sour, has undervalued creative-field thinking, and has discouraged all but the most powerfully independent minds.

Our whole civilization has been the loser. Consider the shake-up at the National Aeronautics and Space Administration after the explosion of the space shuttle *Challenger* in January 1986. Investigative study revealed that control of the agency was in the hands of people whose thinking was so linear, so oriented toward their particular level on the vertical chain of command, that they lost sight of the overall purpose of their organization: safe, effective, reliable transit to space and back again. And this is not to mention the awful loss of human feeling for the people who were strapped into that shuttle. Each level of command tended to see itself as discrete, as separate from the rest, so that it did not seem important to communicate to top-level decision makers the concerns expressed lower down the chain. To me, the brilliant gold and white explosion against the blue skies over Cape Canaveral is a symbol of the destructive power of linear ("bright") thinking to the exclusion of global ("dark") thinking and the inclusive communication it brings in its wake. Work gets done more slowly with a "darker," consensus-seeking, more traditionally "feminine" organizational style: but the chances of sudden destruction are significantly reduced.

EDITING OUT HALF OF BIBLICAL POLARITIES

I do not blame Christianity for the entire left-brain, linear emphasis of Western education; but I do claim that had Christian leaders paid sufficient attention to the whole spectrum of biblical imagery, Christianity could have been part of the solution instead of intensifying the problem. Our attitudes toward other people and also toward our own feelings and inner process are adversely affected when we pick up only *one* aspect of biblical imagery that is actually *multifaceted*. Before we look more closely at the damage caused, let's examine how Christianity has edited out an unwanted half of biblical images.

Job 38:29 depicts the divine voice from the whirlwind asking Job a rhetorical question: "Out of whose womb came the ice?" The passage associates God with coldness rather than warmth, and with female anatomy (gynomorphic imagery) rather than with the masculine or androcentric imagery still heard from Christian pulpits almost everywhere.

According to the ancient theory of four bodily "humors" in correspondence with the four basic elements—earth, air, fire, and water—coldness is a quality common to the two "feminine" and material elements of earth and water, while heat is common to the "masculine" and spiritual elements of air and fire.[5] Hence, when we see the Bible associating God with coldness, we know that the association is also with matter or body as opposed to spirit, and with female as opposed to male—in short, to darkness as opposed to light (warmth). And the Book of Job is not the only spot where God is associated with coldness and materiality. Psalm 147 deals very specifically in the God of *both extremes*, who "giveth snow like wool," who "scattereth the hoar frost like ashes," who "casteth forth ice like morsels; who can stand before God's cold?" The same God who sends the ice also melts it, according to the following verse, which returns us to the more customary association of God with warmth. Why have we edited out the coldness images, with all their connections to matter and to femaleness, to darkness? And what have we done to ourselves in the process?

My book on the biblical imagery of God as female, *The Divine Feminine*, discusses this topic in more detail than I can include here. But in order to remind us of the way our obsession with images of Father, King, Husband, and Master has cut us off from the *other* pole of biblical images, let me just mention several passages in which the intention seems to be to force our minds to grasp a simultaneous polarity of masculine and feminine within the nature of God. Job 38:29 makes a good place to start, because the question about God's womb making the ice is followed immediately by another question: "And the hoary frost of heaven, who hath gendered it?" The sexual imagery is unmistakable: God has a womb in which She makes the ice, but simultaneously God is the male who engenders the hoary frost of heaven within that womb. Why has the church tended to edit out the female half of this set of parallel questions?

Similarly, in Psalm 123:2 the Psalmist speaks of God in parallel andromorphic and gynomorphic images:

> Behold, as the eyes of servants look unto the hand of their masters, and as the eyes of a maiden unto the hand of her mistress; so our eyes wait upon [the Sovereign One] our God, until that [God] have mercy upon us.

This passage strongly implies that each of us needs a same-sex role model in order to know how to behave; and by comparing human role models to human dependency upon God as a role model, the Psalmist suggests one particular way in which women have been impoverished by the church's use of exclusively andromorphic images of God. We have been deprived of our powerful same-sex role model in heaven.

There are a few other places where in a single passage the Hebrew Scriptures speak of God as playing both the masculine and feminine roles in the creation of new life;[6] and there are numerous other places where God is spoken of in unmistakably female images without parallel male images.[7] So Jesus had solid precedent for what Luke's Gospel depicts him as doing: telling stories that alternately show God in androcentric and in gynocentric imagery. In Luke 15, for instance, we are told that Jesus presented three parables to the Pharisees who were upset about his hobnobbing with sinners. The first parable is of the shepherd who seeks the one lost sheep rather than being satisfied with the ninety-nine that are safe in the sheepfold. Although all the shepherds I've ever seen in Bible illustrations were male, Gen. 29:9 informs me that Rachel was a shepherd. Nothing in the passage indicates that people in her society thought it unusual for a woman to be doing that job. So the first parable in Luke 15 uses shepherd imagery for God, imagery which could be either gynocentric or androcentric. The second parable depicts God as the woman seeking her lost coin, an explicitly gynocentric image. And the third parable depicts God as the unconditionally loving father who welcomes home his bedraggled ne'er-do-well son, an androcentric image but a countercultural one, since it is the mother who is traditionally expected to be unconditionally loving. Why has the church forgotten the gynocentric images and focused only on the masculine imagery of God? Apart from the political reasons, could it be because femaleness, like coldness, has been too closely associated with the darkness that Christians have for centuries attempted to deny?

THE JUNGIAN CRITIQUE OF CHRISTIANITY

Carl Jung has been very critical of Christianity because it has split itself away from darkness and all that darkness represents.[8] In *Aion*, for instance, Jung commented:

> In the empirical Self, light and shadow form a paradoxical unity. In the Christian concept, on the other hand, the archetype is hopelessly split into two irreconcilable halves, leading ultimately to a metaphysical dualism—the final sep-

aration of the kingdom of heaven from the fiery world of the damned.[9]

The passages already quoted from *Dictionary of the New Testament* show that Jung is not overstating the case. I remember my own Protestant fundamentalist upbringing, in which I was *robbed of mystery* by being force-fed neat answers before I was old enough to have any feel for the questions, ambiguities, and mysteries of human experience. The God I was taught to worship was old, rich, one-hundred percent healthy and ablebodied, heterosexual, masculine, and totally good. I was a very poor match for that model, but that was okay because God was Totally Other than I was, anyhow. I was taught to distrust my own experience and to strive to love this Totally Other, totally perfect Being who had created me in His image, but whose image I had heedlessly and disobediently destroyed in myself.

Desperately and doggedly, I tried to be *perfect* in order more fully to resemble Jesus Christ, the antiseptically perfect Son of the God I worshiped. And the older I got, the more desperate I became. I realized that even my virtues were intertwined with what most people would call my vices. To rid myself of vice would be to rid myself of virtue as well! By the time I reached middle age, the burden of my sins was inescapable and truly intolerable.

What a relief, then, to discover that my true goal is not to be *perfect*, but merely to be *whole*, to be perfectly *myself*, made in the image of a God who is *not* Totally Other, but rather is all encompassing, encompassing even me, *within* me as well as far beyond what I can grasp or understand! What a relief to discover that I am *rooted* in the divine nature so inseparably that none of my delusions of separateness could ever be able to separate me even one little bit from the nature of God! What a relief to realize that roots grow and thrive in *dirt*, in the moist cold darkness of the earth, and therefore suggest that God, the Ground of our Being and Becoming, is *darkness* as well as light!

In *The Illness That We Are*, subtitled *A Jungian Critique of Christianity*, psychoanalyst John P. Dourley has pointed out that the three major absences in the Christian myth are "the realities of matter, woman, and evil" (p. 73). These absences in turn contribute to traditional Christianity's exclusiveness and triumphalism in relation to other religions. As Dourley puts it, "the spirit of Jung's thought, based on his understanding that the psyche's energies naturally move toward totality, demands that any religion claiming to have a monopoly on a final exhaustive revelation must eventually come to some saving doubt and humanizing relativization of such a claim" (p. 73). That saving relativization can come about only when Christians enter the dark cloud of unknowing concerning God and come to value mystery and darkness, a mystery that leaves room for the approaches taken by other religions. (The brightly lit rationalism of American fundamentalism, in which the Bible is understood to offer clear-cut answers to everything, allows for no darkness at all! Darkness is the wholly other, to be either repudiated or else converted into light).

It is important to recognize that all of the major elements that traditional Christianity *lacks*, from the Jungian perspective, may be subsumed under the single heading of darkness. Matter has always been associated with darkness rather than light; and certainly we Christians need to develop a new materialism, a new appreciation for the surfaces and embodiment of things, what Susan Sontag has called an "erotics of art" as opposed to a tendency to leap instantly into interpretative thoughts *about* things. Similarly, women have always been associated with darkness, especially in the Protestant tradition, where there has been no veneration of the Blessed Virgin Mother to keep our spirits in touch with the ancient Great Mother of us all. Evil has been associated with darkness as well, with the result that we Christians have tried to split ourselves off from our own depressions, fears, angers, doubts, and griefs— from all that we sometimes refer to as our "black moods." And, as I have implied earlier, our horror of darkness has continually aided and abetted our sin of white racism.

Our everyday language reflects both our racism and our fear of darkness that has crippled us. For instance, to be excluded from a club is to be "blackballed"; to be in disgrace is to be a "black sheep"; financial failure occurred on black Friday; an unlucky day is a black-letter day; extortion is blackmail; to defy the law is to raise the black flag; evil magic is black magic, as opposed to good or white magic; and since the cold, misty, dark Easter Monday in 1360, when Edward III lost many of his soldiers and horses in a hailstorm, the day after Easter has been called Black Monday. Satan is frequently referred to as the Black Man.[10]

POSITIVE BIBLICAL IMAGES OF DARKNESS

If it is true that we Western Christians have erred in our attempts to split ourselves off from darkness, then we might expect to find positive and neglected images of darkness in the Bible, images that preachers and lay people could lift up in everyday discourse in an attempt to move ourselves and all of our society toward wholeness. And, indeed, there are such images.

Isaiah tells us plainly that God says, "I am [the Sovereign One], and there is none else. I form the light, and create the darkness: I make peace, and create evil: I [the Sovereign One] do all these things" (45:6–7). And the first chapter of Genesis makes clear that darkness is the matrix out of which the whole created universe is drawn: "Darkness was upon the face of the deep." (Incidentally, this verse has not one but three images associated with the unconscious mind—darkness, depth, and water). Moving over this primeval deep dark water, God differentiates light from darkness and then places the two of them into the synthesis of a single "day."

Human creativity has followed a similar sequence ever since:

> Beginning with undifferentiated knowledge and experience, the creator (poet or artist of any sort) proceeds through differentiation and joining, expansion and constriction, stray pathways and returns, diffusions and sharpenings, fantasy and reality, world visions and narrow technical concerns, cultural concerns and individual preoccupations, art styles and personal styles, [passionate] arousal and ratiocination, abstraction and concretion, breaking and making. Always, as there are factors and processes tending toward diffusion and expansion, there are equally strong factors and processes directed toward differentiation and joining.[11]

Always there is the dark matrix, the differentiation of light and darkness, and the constant interplay of light and darkness in the succession of nights and days. And always there is the fact that it takes darkness as well as light to make up the single twenty-four-hour period we designate as a calendar day. How much healthier we would be if we were able to relax about the interplay of light and darkness within our own beings and within our relationships!

Not only does biblical imagery suggest that darkness is the matrix of all creation and in constant and necessary alternation with light, so that one day is a *synthesis* of light and darkness; the Bible also repeatedly suggests that darkness is the dwelling place of God as surely as light is. In the tabernacle, the ark of the testimony was covered with a veil (Exod. 40:21), and the Holy of Holies was set off by a veil that must have plunged the place into pitch darkness as the context for the Shekinah glory. When God met with Moses on Mount Sinai, the mountain was covered by a thick cloud that signified the divine presence (Exod. 19:16). David's song of deliverance describes God's making darkness into pavilions surrounding God's Self, "dark waters, and thick clouds of the skies" (2 Sam. 22:12), and Solomon declared that God had spoken about dwelling in the thick darkness (1 Kings 8:12). Psalm 18:11 utilizes similar imagery, telling us that God "made darkness [God's] secret place; [God's] pavilion round about . . . [was] dark waters and thick clouds of the skies." If "clouds and darkness are round about God," as Psalm 97:2 asserts, why then have we focused so exclusively upon the light that we have become quite literally afraid of our own shadows?

Victorian poet Alfred, Lord Tennyson, was the first to make me realize the practical implications of the fact that when the children of Israel were in the wilderness, God "went before them by day in a pillar of cloud, to lead them the way; and by night in a pillar of fire, to give them light" (Exod. 13:21). Concerning his beloved friend Arthur Henry Hallam, Tennyson wrote these lines:

> Perplexed in faith, but pure in deeds,
> At last he beat his music out.
> There lives more faith in honest doubt,
> Believe me, than in half the creeds.
> > He fought his doubts and gathered strength,
> > He would not make his judgment blind,
> > He faced the spectors of the mind
> > And laid them, thus he came at length
> To find a stronger faith his own,
> And Power was with him in the night,
> Which makes the darkness and the light,
> And dwells not in the light alone,
> > But in the darkness and the cloud,
> > As over Sinai's peaks of old,

> While Israel made their gods of gold,
> Although the trumpet blew so loud.[12]

Pondering Tennyson's words, I realized that in the case of the wilderness wanderings, God's presence always appeared to the people in the form of the *other*. When it was daylight, God was in the darkness of the pillar of cloud. When it was dark night, God was in the brightness of the pillar of fire. How dangerous, then, for us to reject that which is opposite to what we think ourselves to be—to think ourselves superior to people poorer or richer or darker or lighter or gayer or straighter than we, or to people who think differently from ourselves, or even to aspects of our own experience that we judge to be negative. God's presence may be waiting for us precisely there!

In fact, a passage in Isaiah states that when God causes God's servant to be in darkness, it is dangerous and counterproductive to try to provide light:

> Who among you fears the [Sovereign]
> and obeys the voice of [God's] servant,
> Who walks in darkness
> and has no light,
> Yet trusts in the name of the [Sovereign]
> and relies upon God?
> Behold, all you who kindle a fire,
> who set brands alight!
> Walk by the light of your fire,
> and by the brands which you have kindled!
> This shall you have from my hand:
> you shall lie down in torment.
> (Isa. 50:10–11, RSV; inclusive language mine.)

Better darkness with God's presence and approval, apparently, than flaming torches with God's rage! If I am right that Christianity has erred by trying to apply images of a universal perspective to the everyday, limited experience of human beings, this passage sounds like a judgment upon our error. Many of us have indeed been forced to "lie down in [psychological] torment" because of the brightly lit judgmentalism of our churches.

NEGATIVE BIBLICAL IMAGES ASSOCIATED WITH LIGHT

Along with retrieving positive biblical images of darkness to help break down human judgmentalism, it is also important to retrieve the negative images of brightness or light. The vast preponderance of biblical imagery associates light with all that is perfect and good, as in 1 John 1:5: ". . . God is light and in [God] is no darkness at all." This imagery is so widely utilized that there is no need to repeat it. But it is important to point out that the intensely literalistic unconscious mind has no real problem in slipping from "God is light" to "God is white."

Because the biblical authors so closely associate brightness with holiness, one finds a negative view of light mainly in those images clustered around the sun's heat and the burning of fire. When we remember that the Bible stems from the Middle East where draught and scorching were serious problems, we realize the implications of passages like Isaiah 25:4–5, where God is depicted as "a shade from the heat": here the divine presence is dark and solid (stereotypically female) while the light is dangerous and oppressive. Isaiah goes on to compare "the blast of the ruthless" to "heat in the dry place"; again, cruel pitilessness is compared to the heat associated with the sun's light, a deadly thing in desert areas. And in Jesus' story in Matthew 20:12, the workers who have "borne the burden of the day and scorching heat" are upset at receiving the same wages as those who had been hired only for the cool of the afternoon. Again, the sun is negative; its scorching heat is a burden.

Against this background it is no surprise to find that, according to Revelation 7:16, those who have been purified by the Lamb shall never be struck by the sun, nor by "any scorching heat." The sun with all its light is here viewed as an antagonist, an attacker. Interestingly enough, in the context of this passage, those who are protected from the sun's striking "have washed their robes and made them white in the blood of the Lamb"(7:14). So this one passage contains both negative and positive images of whiteness/brightness/light and its attendant heat.

Similarly, the many biblical images of fire are sometimes positive, sometimes negative. Typical of the negative images are Deuteronomy 9:3, which identifies God as "a devouring fire," and Isaiah 66:16, which says that God executes judgment by fire. When there is fire, there is light; so these images associate brightness with the terrifying anger of God. Imagery of hell may also be a part of this cluster of negative light imagery, although perhaps John Milton is right that the fires of hell give off no light, but only "darkness visible."

Robert Frost is more biblical than he probably knows or cares when, in his poem "Design," he associates whiteness with beautiful symmetry on the one hand and muted horror on the other. The great American novelist Herman Melville did the same thing in his handling of the whiteness of the whale Moby Dick: it is everything godlike, and it is everything demonic as well. How like human beings, with our capacity for godding and our simultaneous capacity for cruel destructiveness! And—dare we think it?—how like God's own internal process as depicted in the Book of Job!

ACCEPTING BOTH LIGHT AND DARKNESS

As long as we are human beings in the world as we know it, we will experience and *need* to experience both the darkness and the light, not only externally but in our own personal moods and relationships as well. In fact, the one experience teaches us to appreciate the other, such as when the expression of anger suddenly clears the air in a relationship and allows the sweetness to flow freely once again. I'd like to make clear that when I write of accepting the dark side of human nature, I am not talking about being as evil as possible, turning knives in other people just to see them writhe. I am talking about the acceptance of our own "dark" feelings —anger, vindictiveness, melancholy, grief, whatever—without editing or repressing them. I am not talking about acting upon all of the feelings: that's where ethics and moral standards come in. Not all feelings should be acted upon, but all feelings should be *felt* rather than denied. Paradoxically, it is by admitting my own vindictive urges that I become less vindictive in my actual behavior. The nastiest people I have ever met are the people with such inflated egos that they cannot allow themselves to acknowledge that they are capable of even the slightest nastiness! And the kindest are those who can recognize that whatever "darkness" human beings can feel is also with their own capability.

A brief poem will illustrate both the positive aspects of darkness and the negative aspects of light. It is an unpublished prayer written by singer and composer Ken Medema. It is addressed to Christ in the form of a mother hen who gathers under the dark safety of her wings all the chicks that are willing to be gathered:

> Come, sweet darkness
> Come, enfold me

Come, my mother
Come and hold me
Give me comfort
Give me shelter
From the burning of the day.

And finally, a personal experience: Some time ago, I
dreamed about falling backward into water. I am so buoy-
ant that in real life I do not sink and can swim underwater
only with tremendous effort. But in the dream I sank with
terrifying velocity down, down, down into the darkness. Just
as I was realizing that I would never be able to make it back
to the surface alive, even if I *could* manage somehow to re-
verse my direction, I saw that instead of getting darker, at
the greatest depth there began to be light. I was sinking rap-
idly through murky darkness into a glorious light! As John
Donne commented centuries ago, "So death doth touch the
resurrection." The dream was prophetic: in the months following it, I went through truly terrifying inner experiences
of darkness and light, experiences calculated to teach me a
more creative, more receptive attitude toward life and my
own psyche than I had previously enjoyed. Nothing in the
theology of my youth ever prepared me for these experiences,
but thanks to feminist theology and black theology, to what
we might call Jungian theology, and to liberation theology
generally, and thanks to God's working in the depths of my
being, I have survived.

As a result of passage through these cold dark waters I
have become a little more balanced, a little more human, a
little more whole, a little more joyous in my attempts at godding. So the darkness was blessed, after all. I ask that the
preachers among my readers lift up the negative biblical imagery of light and the positive biblical imagery of darkness,
with the related imagery of God's femaleness and immanent
embodiedness and the materiality, as a partial antidote to

white racism, sexism, antimaterialism, overemphasis on linear logic, judgmentalism, perfectionism, fear of human sexuality, and accompanying self-deceptions. I ask that we Christian lay people also expand our everyday language to include these little-known biblical images, and for the same reasons. As we remember that God is above and in and through everything and everyone, as we help ourselves to embrace rather than deny darkness, Power will be not only *with* but *in* us in the night: Power that makes the darkness and the light, Power that dwells not in the light alone, but in the darkness and the cloud.

NOTES

1. Rico explains that using the circles is vital because making circles seems foolish to the left, linear, logic-oriented half of the brain—the half that controls the right side of our bodies (the traditionally masculine side). The contempt our left brain feels for little circles allows it to relax and withdraw, so that we can gain access to the darker, more creative right lobe of the brain. Usually when writers are stumped (blocked), it is the logic-oriented linear left side of the brain that is stuck. If we can get in touch with our more intuitive and global ("feminine" and "dark") right lobe, we will usually have plenty to work with. Outlines or lists are too linear and logically organized to have the same effect as clustered circles.

2. *The Norton Anthology of Literature by Women* ed. Sandra M. Gilbert and Susan Gubar (New York: W. W. Norton, 1985), p.133.

3. Vern L. Bullough, *The Subordinate Sex* (Baltimore: Penguin Books, 1974), p. 107.

4. Toni Morrison, *The Bluest Eye*, in *The Norton Anthology of Literature by Women*, pp. 213–14.

5. E. M. W. Tillyard, *The Elizabethan World Picture* (New York: Random House, n.d.), p. 69.

6. Most notably Deuteronomy 32:18.

7. For these, see Virginia Ramey Mollenkott, *The Divine Feminine* (New York: Crossroad, 1983).

8. My discussion of Jung and Christianity is deeply indebted to John P. Dourley, *The Illness That We Are: A Jungian Critique of Christianity* (Toronto: Inner City Books, 1984).

9. *The Collected Works of Carl Jung*, Vol. 9 (Princeton: Princeton University Press, 1953), ii, paragraph 76.

10. See William Rose Benet, *The Reader's Encyclopedia*, Vol. 1 (New York: Thomas Y. Crowell, 1948), pp. 113–14.

11. Albert Rothenberg, M.D., *The Emerging Goddess:The Creative Process in Art, Science, and Other Fields* (Chicago: The University of Chicago Press, 1979), p. 370.

12. *In Memoriam*, Section 96, stanzas 3–6.

5

Godding and Sexual Identity

According to Scripture, the lifestyles of Christian people—including our sexual identities—are matters of great importance. For instance, we are told that "when anyone is united to Christ, there is a new world; the old order has gone, and a new order has already begun" (2 Cor. 5:17, NEB). This means, surely, that every aspect of human life is intended to undergo a conversion, a metanoia, a reorientation of life from "old age" patterns to "new age" ones. Believers are intended to embody God's image in the world we inhabit.

From the perspective of the New Creation, everything looks different, because we are in a position to experience God's grace in our bodily lives and to "draw down," "draw in," or "draw up" God's grace to the world as a healing corrective for social ills. Whether we prefer to think of drawing · *down* God's grace, or drawing it *into* human experience, or drawing it *up* from the deepest core of our beings, is a matter of which metaphor we find meaningful. In turn, our metaphoric preference depends upon the way we experience God (and vice versa). The important factor is not which metaphor we prefer, but that we experience God's grace and become transformers or conduits of that grace into the world.

Paul gives us some specifics about being united to Christ in the words that follow his announcement of a new order. "God was in Christ reconciling the world to [God's Self]," we are told; and now in a similar way God

has entrusted us with the message of reconciliation. We come therefore as Christ's ambassadors. It is as if God were appeal-

> ing to you through us; in Christ's name, we implore you, be
> reconciled to God!"

And then Paul takes us a step farther: not only is it *as if* God were speaking through us; God does *in fact* speak through us, because the life, death, and resurrection of Jesus the Christ, the Anointed One, has created a union between the divine and human natures. Paul puts it this way: "Christ was innocent of sin, and yet for our sake God made [Christ] one with human sinfulness, so that in [Christ] we might be made one with the goodness of [God's very Self]". Therefore, says Paul, we are actually sharing in God's work—which I take to mean that we are intended to be cocreators with God in a ministry of healing and reconciliation. Jesuit poet Gerard Manley Hopkins expressed the idea this way: "I am what [Christ] was, because [Christ] was what I am." But whereas Hopkins said we would be like the Christ only in our resurrected bodies, Paul is saying in 2 Corinthians 5 that we people of faith already *are* one with the Goodness of God's very Self *even now* in our mortal bodies and our mortal lifestyles.

On this basis, Paul makes an appeal to the reader: "You have received the grace of God; do not let it go for nothing." Letting God's grace "go for nothing" would entail a failure to transform the currents of God's grace into voltages the modern world is able to receive. As Peter tells us, God's intention is that we human beings may "come to share in the very being of God" (2 Pet. 1:4, NEB). Human lifestyles are intended to be lit up with the light of God's unconditional love.

Although the terminology of Paul and Peter is specifically Christian, I am convinced that their vision includes any person who wants to live significantly. To be "in Christ" is to remember our union with the One who sent us, as Jesus did, and to seek to do God's will as Jesus did. The point here is not cognitive agreement with a set of doctrines and terms, but the embodiment of Jesus' vision in our lifestyles. In a sense, the Christ is the elder brother or sister who has gone before us to demonstrate the way, and yet who walks within us to illuminate the way.

EARTHLY SPIRITUALITY

What all this might mean in terms of human embodiment is clarified by these words from James Nelson's book *Between Two Gardens*[1]: "if we do not know the gospel in our bodies, we do not know the gospel. We either experience God's presence *in our bodies* or not at all" (p. 18). Human beings, as Nelson explains, are neither spirits nor bodies but a union of the two; we are "embodied spirits" or "spirited bodies" (p. 169). Spiritual life is therefore intended to involve the *totality* of our selves, including and perhaps especially our sexual selves. Sexuality is so involved in the center of our lives, so intertwined with our creativity, that when the power of our sexuality is crippled by self-rejection, all of our cocreatorship with God is crippled and thwarted.

By sexuality I mean, of course, much more than genital activity. In its broadest and deepest meaning, our sexuality *is* our embodied spirit, that aspect of ourselves that experiences a need for intimate communion with other people and with God. Our sexuality includes our emotional yearning, our cognitive yearning to know the other, our physical and spiritual hunger for community. Sexuality includes what Adam and Eve felt toward each other as they walked with God and made love in Eden and were naked and were not ashamed. Only after they had distrusted God's provision for them and had become alienated from God's loving spirit at the depths of their own beings, only then did they begin to express distrust of their sexual intimacy and vulnerability. There was no male supremacy in the Garden of Eden until that self-alienation. The misuse of human sexuality in a pattern of male dominance and female submission is depicted in Genesis 3 as inner alienation from God's Spirit as the ground of the human spirit. Patriarchal dominance is an expression of the fear of intimacy, the fear of being vulnerable, and ultimately the fear of love. So, for that matter, is irresponsible passivity and submission.

Fortunately for the human condition, Jesus became one with human experience without forgetting human groundedness in God's Spirit. Hence the rest of us in turn may be restored to wholeness within the Christ-nature, defined by Paul as the new nature of the New Humanity in the New Creation: "When anyone is united to Christ, there is a new world, the old order has gone, and a new order has already begun."

SEXUALITY IN THE NEW CREATION

For centuries we have been living in a patriarchy that, according to Genesis, results from the distrust of God's love as the Source and Energizer and Essence of our deepest nature. But in accepting our union with the Christ-nature, that is, in affirming our willingness to do God's will, we become the New Humanity in which are dissolved all the barriers of racism, classism, sexism, heterosexism, and the militarism that grows out of them (see Gal. 3:28). We are then in a position to "draw down" or "draw up" or "draw in" God's grace to our world, to embody in our lifestyles the unconditional love of God the Cosmic Lover. Our contemporaries need to hear the Good News that God the Lover graciously accepts *all* of our sexual dimensions—our yearnings and fantasies, our bodily feelings, our irresponsibilites, our yearnings for sexual responsibility, the whole works! (It is not, alas, the message that our contemporaries have been hearing from the church as a whole.)

I would not like to be understood as saying that "anything goes," and that "if it feels good, do it." I fully recognize that sexual power, like any great power, needs to be disciplined and channeled toward a responsible and loving expression. But I want to agree heartily with James Nelson that human beings "share in God's work" precisely within our sweating, yearning, orgasmic (or inorgasmic) bodies. And of course our ministry of reconciliation is to other people precisely with *their* sweating, yearning, orgasmic (or inorgasmic) bodies. Spirituality is not and indeed cannot be disembodied.

Human beings can be "Christlike" only because Jesus was fully human. He was identified as "the firstborn among *many* [sisters and] brothers" (Rom. 8:29). This fact of Scripture led Irenaeus, second-century Bishop of Lyons, to write a hymn that offers this challenge:

> I became man for thee:
> You become god for me.
> If you do not, if you do not
> Then you betray me.[2]

And that challenge, of course, is the topic of this book. If we attempt to deny or reject our human embodiment with all the tensions it produces, we thwart our ability to be Christlike, to "god," or, in Paul's terms, to share "God's work" in this world.

At the college where I teach, I often watch students and faculty streaming across campus and think about all the private hopes, fears, joys, and sufferings they represent. And I wonder why people so often make life more difficult than it needs to be by judgmentalism and cruelty. I believe that instead of adding burdens onto the shoulders of other people, Christian lifestyles are intended to embody a message of liberation. It was not to enslave that Jesus came, but to set free.

And by the way we live, we Christians are Christ's ambassadors to our culture, for good or ill. No wonder people have no interest in the realm we represent, if we are sour, dour ambassadors!

THE CONTRIBUTION OF INTIMATE RELATING

Our intimate relationships can be signals of the liberating message that patriarchal us-verus-them categories are not God's will, and that the fearsome militaristic results of us-versus-them thinking are not God's will either. By intentionally opening our minds daily to the radiance of God the Cosmic Lover, and by working hard to discipline our egotism and learning to negotiate honestly with each other, we can beam to our contemporaries the good news that our becoming a New Humanity is God's will, that relationships of respectful mutuality are God's will, that a human community which affirms diversity is God's will, that there is enough for all of us when we live cooperatively rather than competitively, and that supportive mutuality is God's intention for humankind. In other words, right relationship with God is expressed primarily through right relationship with other people. Better one solid, honest love relationship in which we empower each other to take off our psychological masks, and in which we uphold an image of justice through mutuality—better that than an impersonal, abstract, and inflated attempt to love thousands of people through lofty gestures that lack precision and embodied reality!

The thing about one concrete interpersonal relationship is that, as time goes by, the relationship always forces us to deal with the dual poles of attachment and autonomy on which all love relationships turn. Males in our society have been socialized to value autonomy and to fear attachment. Females have been taught the opposite: to value attachment and to fear autonomy. But whether we are male or female, all of us have a need for autonomy—for fulfilling our own desires and for taking charge of our own destinies; and all of us, female or male, have a need for attachment, for a sense of connectedness and mutual response-ability. When we see ourselves as ambassadors of God's love only in the sense of speaking from pulpits to dozens or hundreds or thousands of people, only in a theorizing abstract sense, we do not have to get down to work on the relational tensions between attachment and autonomy. Similarly, when one person dominates the other, the attachment-autonomy tension is never resolved, because the dominant person calls the shots. For these reasons it seems vital to me that our spiritual outreach be rooted firmly in intimate egalitarian relationships of mutuality. I am not saying that the relationship must be genital, but I *am* saying that intimate vulnerability to another person or a group of persons in community keeps us grounded and helps us avoid inflated ideas about our own grandeur. We need community to help us get wise to ourselves. I do not believe that "microcosmic love" and "macrocosmic love" are mutually exclusive, but if they were, I would choose "microcosmic love" every time.

TWO DEFINITIONS OF SIN

In this connection, it is interesting to think about the traditional Christian definition of sin as opposed to the definition of sin that has emerged from liberation theology. Traditionally, sin has been defined as selfish pride, a tendency to regard oneself as the ultimate reality, a tendency to use other people as though they were only objects created to meet one's own needs as subject. This seems a very accurate definition of sin when applied to those who are either financially or physically stronger and thus normative over others. But when it is preached by a dominant group to subordinate groups, it becomes an ugly distortion of reality. Every attempt the subordinates make to achieve greater autonomy is interpreted by the normative group as selfish pride—despite the fact that the subordinates are merely trying to attain a status the "normatives" already possess!

For instance, many American women in recent decades have realized that their claims to individualism (in an individualistic culture) have been denied "on behalf of biological or spiritual determinism that relegates [women] to the realm of nature rather than autonomous will."[3] For this reason, feminist aspirations often take a highly individualistic form, and religious pundits have been quick to label those aspirations shamefully selfish. But the fact is that having internalized society's relegation of them to natural determinism, these same women had tended to consider everybody's needs *except* their own. They had been so eager to maintain connectedness to everybody else that many acted as if they were created solely to meet everybody else's need. Now that such women are learning to factor themselves into the equations of need, the *last* thing they need to hear is that they should repent of their prideful alienation from others!

What any oppressed person needs to repent of is not pride, but lack of it! Girls and women in our culture need to turn away from self-denigration and learn to respect and develop their own gifts. Many peasants in Latin America have discovered a need to let go of passivity in the face of poverty, recognizing God's love for them and their entitlement to the good basics of life. To preach Christlike servanthood to people who have never been in touch with their power and autonomy, is to commit an obscenity. First, people must be empowered as, for instance, Dom Helder Camara has empowered the slum dwellers of Brazil. Only after empowerment can people be shown that according to Jesus, the proper use of power is to use it to empower others. You cannot choose to give up power or use it to serve others until you *have the power to choose!* Each one of us has areas where we are powerful and areas where we are oppressed. The Gospel speaks empowerment to our oppressed aspects, and repentance and responsibility to our powerfulness.

CONSTRUCTIVE VERSUS DESTRUCTIVE SELF-IDENTIFICATION

I believe there is a "constructive self-interest" and a "destructive self-interest." The difference between them is the way we identify the self. All of us are born into a skin-encapsulated body-self, and our first job as we grow to maturity is to define ourselves, to learn what gifts we have, and to develop ourselves into all we possibly can be. To do this is to get in touch with our personal power, our autonomy, our capacity to make meaningful choices. This is constructive self-interest. But for a mature human being, this autonomy is never an end in itself. It is also necessary to reach out to others, to use one's gifts responsibly, to learn to live in community, to learn about healthy attachment and connectedness. When we have reached out and connected, we no longer define ourselves simply as a separate entity, but rather as a body-self in community. A Christian way of saying this is that we must learn to be subject to one another out of reverence for Christ—out of reverence, that is, for the whole of the New Humanity. This, too, is constructive self-interest, in that we meet our own needs in a communally responsible context.

Destructive self-interest, by contrast, is to mean *only* my skin-encapsulated ego, my own personality and individual body-self, when I say "me." Constructive self-interest is to mean my larger identity when I speak of "self"—including my connectedness to God and all of God's creatures. Constructive self-interest recognizes that if I win an argument over you, we both lose because my dominance diminishes our intimacy. Constructive self-interest knows that it is in my own best interest to find a way to which both of us are fulfilled and satisfied, so that our intimacy can be strengthened rather than diminished.

Nuclear weapons have brought the world to the point where the interdependence of security interests must govern international relationships if the human race hopes to survive. As Carl Sagan remarked during the televised discussion that followed the broadcast of the film *The Day After*, the one thing we can count on the Soviet Union to do is to serve its own best interests. And the possibility of the total annihilation of human life on this planet will, please God, teach all nations that our own best interests lie in the direction of mutual cooperation rather than in further competition.

I see a relationship between international politics and politics within the "private" family unit. Mutually supportive relationships are peacemaking in that they contribute to a planetary paradigm shift away from the patriarchal model of individualistic domination toward a liberating new model of mutuality. Therefore, our family relationships are not simply private after all: they are political models. Either they radiate justice and wholeness into our world or else they contribute to fragmentation and destructive alienation.

EXPANDING THE CONCEPT OF FAMILY

Careful readers have no doubt noticed that in discussing primary relationships I have specified neither marriage nor the nuclear family. According to the 1980 United States Census Bureau Report on Household and Family Characteristics, only about ten percent of all American households consist of the "normative" model: husband and wife with two or more children at home and the husband the sole wage earner. Politicians who support only that model when they describe themselves as "pro-family" should alert themselves to the fact that they are serving only a small minority of the public. A truly "pro-family" stance would be supportive of all the many forms that human bonding takes in our culture, the many forms of "family." Among these forms of family would be trial marriages; covenant relationships that have no legal status; families merged through remarriage; same sex unions, with or without children; childless couples; an adult with aging parents; single-parent families; communities of adults who share neither blood ties nor genital intimacy, but who constitute families nevertheless because of the covenant among the members; and so forth. To be "pro-family" in a reconciling way is to affirm family in all of its pluralism.

People who are interested in godding would be wise to cease evaluating sexual relationships on the basis of their object or their legal sanctions and evaluate them instead on the basis of their relational quality. As we all know or ought to know, horrible sins have been committed within the context of fully sanctioned heterosexual marriage: rape, incest, battering of the body and the spirit. Beautiful and supportive mutual relationships have been sustained both with and without benefit of clergy and between two men or two women as well as by heterosexual couples. In this connection, it is wise to remind ourselves that specifically Christian marriage liturgies do not make their appearance until the ninth century, and the Catholic Church did not absolutely require a marriage liturgy until the latter part of the sixteenth century! It is also instructive to learn that despite the probable efforts to destroy such evidence, a Roman Catholic liturgy consecrating the union of two male clerics has survived from the eighth century.[4] By contrast, the "normative" family model in which the mother stays home with the children is a nineteenth-century development. We could do society a big favor by ceasing to elevate into a norm the model of the most recent family unit.

For that matter, Jesus himself did not have a very favorable view of biological families in general, possibly because he saw that they tended to put women and unmarried adults into secondary roles. When well-meaning people tried to define Jesus in terms of his biological family, he insisted that his real family ties were with those who had heard the Word of God and had kept it as the basis of their lifestyles (see, for example, Matt. 12:46–50, 19:29; Mark 3:21). In other words, Jesus defined his own family in terms of *intentional covenant* rather than in terms of biological or legal relatedness. That's particularly interesting because society has forced gay men and lesbians to define their families in terms of intentional covenant rather than legal relatedness, but has then punished them for failing to be a biological family by depriving them of tax breaks, prestige, and various social privileges. If they value the experience of Jesus, at least they're in good company!

It is ironic that so many churches that claim to follow Jesus have been exceedingly hostile to any lifestyle that does not fit into the model of heterosexual marriage. Widespread Christian suspicion of communal living is downright amusing in the light of the fact that Jesus ministered from within such a community, traveling with an extensive group of male and female disciples (Luke 8:1–3).

BIBLICAL PLURALISM CONCERNING FAMILY

As a matter of fact, the Bible depicts a great variety of family lifestyles, almost as great as the variety we see within contemporary culture. Attention to the text of Scripture will give very little support to the religious right's obsession with the family in which mother stays home with the children. Take, for one instance, the genealogy of Jesus that is presented in the Gospel of Matthew. It is of course a great honor to be listed in the family line of "Jesus Christ the [child] of David, the [child] of Abraham." Forty-one males are mentioned in this genealogy, and only five females. The fascinating fact is that each of the five women is associated with some sort of sexual irregularity. Not one of them fits neatly into the patterns of patriarchal, husband-controlled heterosexual marriage. Tamar is mentioned: Tamar who had to pretend to be a prostitute in order to force her neglectful father-in-law to let her raise up children for her deceased husband (Gen. 38:1–29). Rahab is mentioned—and Rahab was not only a prostitute but had the nerve to commit civil disobedience against her own country by casting her lot with the spies from Israel (Josh. 2:1–24, 6:22–25). Ruth is mentioned— Ruth who bonded herself with her mother-in-law in a covenant that is often used in marriage ceremonies, and who slept with Boaz on the threshing floor in order to pressure him into doing his duty by marrying her. (We must not let ourselves be deceived by the euphemism about uncovering his feet. Ruth "made it" with Boaz!) Bathsheba is not mentioned by name, but is mentioned only as "Uriah's wife," perhaps because she is the most passive and acted-upon of the five women in Christ's genealogy. Bathsheba is, of course, the woman King David stole from Uriah, the loyal soldier, whom David then sent into the front line of battle so that he would be killed. Bathsheba took her most active role when she pressured David in his old age to keep his promise to name their son Solomon as his successor. And finally there is the Blessed Virgin Mary, the unwed mother who voluntarily risked societal rejection and from whom was born Jesus, who is called the Christ.

I mention all this because I think Matthew's genealogy of

Jesus has important implications for those people whom Christians stigmatize as sexually irregular. Because the Bible reflects the patriarchal culture out of which it was given to us, women are not usually mentioned in its genealogies. But all of the five women who are singled out for mention in this tremendously honorable context were not only stigmatized by the "original sin" of being female; they were also involved in sexual irregularities; and furthermore, most of them were involved in pressuring men to the performance of duties the men had neglected. The Blessed Virgin Mary is an exception here only because Joseph was so willing to play the secondary and supportive, stereotypically "feminine" role into which he was cast by the birth of Jesus. All honor to Joseph, the first male feminist of the Christian era!

Certainly Matthew's genealogy implies that people of faith ought to be far more pluralistic than we have formerly been. If we *must* evaluate relationships, including sexual relationships, they ought to be evaluated in terms of their whole-life context, not by whether they are with the same sex or the other sex, or whether they take place within legal and religious sanctions. The big question is: Does the relationship engender God's grace within human embodiment? Do I and my friend or my partner or my spouse empower each other to share in God's grace? Is our relationship in and of itself a sharing of God's grace through honest mutual respect and loving supportiveness? Nothing that we do can be more important than embodying the gracious unconditional love of God in relationship to another human being or beings.

PUBLIC STANCE AND PRIVATE ACTION

In this connection, I am reminded of the film *Gandhi*. As one reviewer put it (I think in *Sojourners* magazine), this film "showed us the way out of hell" by illustrating for us the way to break the cycle in which structural violence breeds the counterviolence of the oppressed, and that violence breeds the violence of repression. And yet in his personal relationship with his wife, Gandhi was guilty of psychological violence, insisting that his wife live up to his vision of reality by cleaning latrines and thus violating India's caste system. Gandhi himself admitted that he had imposed his vision of reality upon his wife; in my opinion, this was a form of violence. I say this not in order to deny the great contribution that Gandhi made to human civilization, but only to suggest that, ideally, our lifestyles should embody their public stance even in the most private of our acts. To the degree that Gandhi bullied his wife, his private life belied his public stance of nonviolence. Perhaps his example indicates how difficult it is to have a broad public ministry while being whole on the more private interpersonal plane. Yet the one is not more important than the other. To our quantity-oriented eyes, perhaps, public fame and great accomplishment may seem worth any amount of private alienation. But in the spiritual realm that lies at the very core of our body-selves, it is quality and not quantity that counts. It is vitally important to work as Gandhi did for the modification of unjust and dehumanizing structures. But it is just as important to live as honestly, lovingly, gracefully, and respectfully as we can in our "private" relationships. On every level of life, godding bears witness that the union with Christ brings about "a new world"; that "the old order is gone, and a new order has already begun."

NOTES

1. (New York: Pilgrim Press, 1983).
2. The hymn was played in a tape-recorded version, as part of

Rosemary Crow's *Holy Silence,* by Lutheran pastor Robin Mattison at the Lutheran Theological Conference for Women, Redwood City, California, June 15, 1986.

3. Rosalind Pollack Petchesky, *Abortion and Women's Choice: The State, Sexuality, and Reproductive Freedom* (Boston: Northeastern University Press, 1985), p. 373. Petchesky's work constitutes an excellent wholistic analysis of reproductive politics.

4. John Boswell, Yale historian and author of *Christianity, Social Tolerance, and Homosexuality,* discovered this liturgy and is preparing it for publication.

6

"External" Guidance for Godding

There is a danger in knowing that God is within us, acting through us whenever we are acting out of our most profound core (in which is located the light that nothing has ever been able to extinguish). The danger is that we may become heady, acting as if we need no guidance or advice other than that which comes from our inner light. And indeed, we would need no other guidance if our perceptions of the light were never skewed. As Milton's Jesus says in *Paradise Regained*:

> [One] who receives
> Light from above, from the fountain of light,
> No other doctrine needs.... (bk. 4, lines 288–90)

Because he was a Puritan who had committed civil disobedience by supporting the execution of Charles I and had nearly lost his own life for it during the Restoration of Charles II, Milton had thought a lot about internal and "external" authority. In his great closet-drama *Samson Agonistes*, Milton depicts the Old Testament hero getting himself into serious trouble because he became careless about whether the "inner impulse" to which he responded was coming from God or from his own egotistical desires. When Samson broke the law recorded in Deuteronomy 7:1–3 by marrying "the daughter of an Infidel," his parents were very upset because, as Samson muses:

> they knew not
> That what I motion'd was of God; I knew
> From intimate impulse
> (lines 221–23)

But after the violent end of that marriage, Samson wanted to marry yet another non-Israelite, Dalila. This time, however, the motive came from his own self-destructive ego. Sitting blinded in a Philistine prison, Samson admits that he had misjudged the validity of the impulse: "I thought it lawful from my former act" (line 231). That is, of course, precisely the danger of breaking an important law out of loyalty to a higher law: as long as we are human, we are subject to errors of perception.

And yet, who is to say that God's work was not done, even through the error that cost Samson his vision and his freedom? Not Milton. Lest readers should assume he is warning them to be mindlessly obedient to the "powers that be," Milton depicts Samson as at first refusing to perform feats of strength at the feast of Dagon, the Philistinian god:

> Thou knowest I am a Hebrew, therefore tell them,
> Our Law forbids at their Religious Rites
> My presence; for that cause I cannot come
> (lines 1319–21)

But not long after, Samson consents to go to the feast—not because of the threats of the Philistine lords, but because, as Samson explains to his friends:

> I begin to feel
> Some rousing motions in me which dispose
> To something extraordinary my thoughts
> (lines 1381–83)

He explains that God "may dispense with me or thee/Present in Temples at Idolatrous Rites/For some important cause"

(lines 1377–79). In other words, God has a right to break
God's own laws, in the form of moving God's human champion to break the laws for an extraordinary purpose. And, of
course, Samson crushes the pillars at the feast, brings the
house down, and destroys the entire ruling class of Israel's
chief enemies.

Hence, in the career of Samson, Milton has depicted both
the danger and the necessity of listening to our own inner experience. It is important to know the Law of God, as Samson
clearly knew it; it is important to obey that Law during the ordinary circumstances of life; but is is equally important to
have the courage to break the Law when we know by the still
small voice within us that God is asking us to do so. We may
pay with our lives, as Samson did, for we are human and subject to all the natural and societal laws that govern human experience. Those who have spent time in jail for civil-rights or
peace demonstrations, or for giving sanctuary to refugees,
could tell us something about the courage of enduring the penalty after having the courage to stand up to systemic inequities.

BIBLICAL ILLITERACY

In contrast to the seventeenth century, when Milton lived,
the problem for thoughtful people in the twentieth century
would not so much be having the courage to break God's
laws as it would be *knowing* God's laws in the first place. My
assumption is that God has made God's Self known to us
through the accumulated wisdom of humankind, through
the sacred books of various religions, and in the Judeo-Christian tradition, supremely through the Bible. Yet America,
predominantly a Judeo-Christian nation, is for the most part
biblically illiterate. How can this be, when millions of Americans flock to churches and synagogues every weekend?

The secularism of many Jews would help to explain the phenomenon from the Jewish perspective; and until Vatican II, Roman Catholics were not encouraged to engage in serious Bible study. But what about Protestant churches, spawned under the Reformers' banner of *Sola Scriptura?* How could generations of mainline Protestants have developed such ignorance of their own holy text?

Perhaps the reason was and is embarrassment at the excessive claims of those who say they have a chapter-and-verse to answer every human query. Or perhaps the Bible was underemphasized because pastors had become discouraged during their seminary days by textual critics who seemed to shred the Bible into so many layers that nothing seemed authoritative anymore. Or perhaps the Bible was underemphasized out of embarrassment at the widespread nineteenth-century use of Scripture to support slavery. At that time the proponents of slavery argued that not only was slavery divinely sanctioned among the Hebrew patriarchs, but it was recognized and approved of by Jesus and the apostles. Most mainline churches would like to forget such abuses as quickly as possible.

Furthermore, when combined with twentieth-century relativism, the fact that the Bible had been used to sanction slavery encouraged the concept that a person could prove *anything* from the Bible. And indeed, people can prove almost anything from the Bible if they are willing to violate various time-honored principles of interpretation. But when people honor the respected and traditionally accepted principles of literary interpretation (hermeneutical principles), certain themes emerge as governing themes, and many eccentric and repressive notions are ruled out by those principles.

Perhaps Bible study was forgotten in mainline churches because of the assumption of religious liberalism that modern people could reach religious truth without any help from Scripture. At any rate, and for whatever reason, serious adult

Bible study was largely forgotten in many mainline congregations. Several generations grew up knowing little about the Bible except for whatever passages regularly turned up in the Sunday morning lectionary and in liturgy. But these passages are by definition taken out of their Scriptural context; and busy pastors apparently despaired of the long hard labor of teaching those contexts. In this way was created a vacuum that allowed, on the one hand, some feminists to say that the Bible is the enemy of women and must be abandoned, and on the other hand, people like Phyllis Schlaffley, Elisabeth Elliot, and Jerry Falwell to say that the Bible teaches that women must be secondary to men in the church and in society. With several generations of mainline churchgoers biblically illiterate for all practical purposes, there were very few voices to convince society that *when wholistically interpreted*, the Bible teaches the full equality and mutual responsibility of women and men in the church, in the family, and in society as a whole.

A WHOLISTIC LITERARY APPROACH TO SCRIPTURE

I approach the Bible not as a specialist in Hebrew or Greek, but simply as a professor of literature in English. I am aware that the Bible was written across many centuries by many different hands, with the Old Testament canon taking a thousand years to be decided. Still, I think there is something to be gained by taking the package as it has been handed down to us and attempting to make sense of it as an organic and living whole. This involves assuming that canonical decisions, however chaotic they may have been, nevertheless had some wisdom to them. Using this approach, let me try to demonstrate my conviction that the Bible is a liberating and empowering book for modern women as well as men.

In the first place, readers must begin by consciously acknowledging the very obvious fact that the Bible is not a magic book. It does not mysteriously translate itself into modern American English at exactly the grade level of reading ability of the person who happens to be looking at it at any given moment. The Bible was written across a period of approximately thirteen centuries, in the Hebrew, Greek, and Aramaic languages, and comes to most of us only through translators. And, of course, all translation involves interpretation. Any interpreter of the Bible has the obligation to learn and to respect the ways in which words, concepts, and images were understood by the biblical authors in their particular cultural contexts. For instance: Only after we have understood what the work *kephalē* ("head") meant to Saint Paul can we interpret what his words about husbandly headship might mean in a twentieth-century context.

To say that we do not need scholarly tools because the Holy Spirit tells us directly what Scripture means is to assume that God is not at work through the many scholars who have painstakingly labored to elucidate the Bible and its backgrounds. It is also to subscribe to the concept of a magic book. Only this time the book is not magically available to *everybody*; it is available only to those who have the inside track with the Holy Spirit. As evangelical scholar Bernard Ramm has written, "although the claim to bypass mere human books and go right to the Bible itself sounds devout and spiritual, [in reality] it is a veiled egotism."[1]

THE MEANINGS OF HEADSHIP

Many conservatives have argued on the basis of Paul's Epistles that the husband is intended by God to be the head of the Christian home, the final arbiter of disputes and the maker

of major policies. Upon investigation, this argument turns
out to be based upon Paul's remarks about headship interpreted through the eyes of people who know that the brain,
located in the head, signals decisions to the rest of the body.
But in the Apostle Paul's day and all the way through the
Middle Ages, people thought that decisions were made in the
heart, not in the head. Remembering that, we realize that
Paul did not mean to say that the husband's headship made
him the decision maker. Had that been Paul's intention, he
would have called the husband the *heart* of the wife.

What then did Paul mean by headship? If we look at the
passage about headship in 1 Corinthians 11:3–16, we see
Paul referring to the story in Genesis 2 of woman being fash-
ioned from the rib or side of Adam (woman came from man,
verse 8). This would lead us to believe that Paul might be
using the word *head* in the sense of source, as we speak of the
head of a river. Woman is man's glory because she came from
man, he argues; but a few verses later he reverses himself by
admitting that "as woman came from man, so also man is
born of woman. But everything comes from God." Hence,
God is the ultimate *head* or *source*, and Paul shifts away from
his former theological argument to a cultural and relativistic
argument about head coverings.

Similarly, in Ephesians 5, when the Ephesians author
speaks about husbandly headship, he does so in the context of
Christ's headship in the church. The husband is instructed to
love the wife "as Christ loved the church and *gave up Christ's
self* for the church." So the message to first-century Christian
husbands is that the structure of their marriage could not be
Christian until they assumed the headship of laying aside
their special privileges as men, giving themselves up for their
wives as Christ gave up Christ's self for the church. Since
society still tends to accord to men special privileges on account of their maleness, the message of Ephesians 5 remains
the same: Christian married men must give up specialness

and love their wives as they love their own bodies, Christian married women must respond with self-giving in return, and married couples like all other Christians must "submit to one another out of reverence for Christ."

Inasmuch as headship entails authority, the Ephesians author is defining authority not in terms of power over another, but in terms of serving the other. Thus Ephesians 5, which has so often been enlisted in support of male dominance, actually teaches something similar to Jesus' comment that "whoever wants to become great among you must be your servant, and whoever wants to be first must be your slave" (Matt. 20:26–27, NIV). By specifying *husbandly* headship, Ephesians addresses the challenge of Christlike servanthood directly to those who held the power in first-century society.

I have been focusing on headship not in order to give a complete exegesis, but only to demonstrate that we can get ourselves in a lot of trouble if we assume that a word like *head* meant to Saint Paul what *we* understand it to mean, the location of the brain, the decision maker for the remainder of the body. Because the Bible is not a magic book, we cannot assume that words meant to biblical authors exactly what they mean to us. So people who have taken the biblical words about headship to mean that men ought to make the decisions for women are violating the time-honored hermeneutical principle that interpreters must respect authors' understandings of words within their own cultural experience.

THE CONTEXTUAL LIMITS OF ANALOGY

Another hermeneutical principle states that a concept must be interpreted within the context supplied by the chapter and book and linguistic structure in which it appears. The Ephesians author compares the husband to Christ and the wife to the church in the context of the Christ's giving up privileges of divinity and dying the death of a slave. To hear some interpreters upholding male supremacy with this passage, you would think the analogy was to the husband as Christ coming in power and great glory to judge the quick and the dead! But an analogy must always stay within its original context. If I should make the analogy that Christians are like eagles because we constantly renew our strength in God, it would be unfair of you to report that I called Christians *predators*. It would indeed be true that I made an analogy between Christians and eagles, and it is true that eagles are predatory birds; but you would be telling a falsehood about what I said because you shifted the context in which I spoke of Christians as eagles. By the same token, people who take the analogy of the husband as Christ in any other context than Christ's voluntary self-giving service are reading the Ephesians passage falsely. Such people violate all respect for context.

SHIFTING THE EMPHASIS OF AN IMAGE

I imagine that the author of Ephesians felt sure that in the image of head and body, he had found an image of mutuality that nobody could ever misunderstand. After all, we might envision a guillotine and ask ourselves which we ourselves would rather give up, our heads or our bodies? We get the point, I hope: without each other, both head and body are dead. It is proof of the previously discussed us-versus-them tendency that society has managed to turn the egalitarian mutuality of the head-and-body image into a hierarchical one-is-ruler-over-the-other image.

In Ephesians 4:15, the Ephesians author instructs all Christians "in all things [to] grow up into [the one] who is the Head, that is, Christ." From this remark we know that the head image was never intended as an image of *power over* the body. Christ is the head; Christ is also the body; and all the members of the body are instructed to grow up into the head by assuming Christedness as responsible adult Christian women and men. Instead of encouraging "men to prideful domination and women to irresponsible passivity," we find that the Scriptures call "both women and men to mutual submission and active discipleship."[2]

CENTRAL OR CONTROLLING THEMES

For centuries church authorites have agreed that no individual passage of Scripture may be interpreted in isolation from the overarching themes of Scripture. Yet many have done exactly that, especially when applying Scripture to nonnormative, silenced groups who are not permitted to answer for themselves. We have already seen one example of noncontextual reading in the displacement of the analogy between the husband and the Christ; perhaps an illustration relating to the whole sweep of Scripture would be helpful.

Some time ago, my mother, a Protestant fundamentalist, somewhat shyly asked me, "Virginia, how can you teach that women and men are equal? Doesn't the Bible say that the woman's desire will be for her husband, and he will rule over her?" I asked my mother what was happening in Genesis 3:16 when that statement was made. Mother responded that the Judge was telling Adam and Eve the results of their sin. I asked her, "Is it the job of modern Christians to try to perpetuate the sinful results of the Fall? Or are we intended to stand fast in the liberty in which Christ has made us free?" Mother saw my point, I think, although she is too attached to her fundamentalist church to think very much about other ways of interpreting the Bible. But she did nod agreement when I reminded her that according to Genesis 1:26–27 Adam and Eve were created together on the sixth day, and that together they were given the creation mandate to take charge of the world in which they found themselves. God's original purpose for the human race was interactive mutuality between women and men; there is no hint of male supremacy in either creation story.

For instance, in Genesis 2, the story of the rib, woman is called the *ezer neged* of man. Hebrew scholar David Freedman translates *ezer neged* as "a power equal to man."[3] In the Hebrew Scriptures the word *ezer* always refers to help coming from a position of power; in fact, almost always it refers to God's help to human beings, as in the Psalms: "I will lift up mine eyes unto the hills. From whence comes my help [*ezer*]? My help [*ezer*] comes from God, who made heaven and earth." So those who have translated *ezer neged* as "helpmeet," and have interpreted it to mean that woman is secondary to man and was created to serve man, are simply wrong. Woman was created a power equal to man, and only sinful alienation introduced male supremacy as well as the many other categories of us-versus-them that were discussed earlier. But the Hebrew prophets called the people back toward justice and universal *shalom*; and the Christian Scriptures show us that "in Christ," in the New Humanity, all the barriers of racism, classism, and sexism are overthrown as we are transformed by the renewing of our minds.

Hence the passage my mother so shyly asked me about, in which Eve was told that her husband would rule over her, is not a prescription for human society but rather a description of the sinful state of a society alienated from God, the ground of all being. When placed within the context of its own chapter and book and the whole sweep of Scripture, it describes the alienation of the old creation from which we are set free as members of the New Humanity.

THE ECCENTRIC VERSUS THE NORMATIVE

Another old and respected hermeneutical principle is this one: that difficult, obscure, and highly unusual biblical passages must never be used to govern the interpretation of clearer and more common themes. For instance, 1 Timothy 2:11–15 is a quirky passage that orders women to be silent because woman "was deceived and became a sinner." It also, in many translations, seems to say that women's salvation will come about through bearing children. Many Bible scholars feel sure that this passage is an interpolation added to 1 Timothy when the church was ensuring its own survival by modeling itself after the Roman patriarchal household. But whether or not it was an interpolation, *had the church obeyed its own hermeneutical principle about unusual and isolated ideas*, this passage would never have been used, as it was, to contradict the powerful and crystal-clear biblical theme of salvation by grace through faith. No obscure comment about salvation by childbearing in one single passage can be used to undercut that often-repeated theme of salvation by grace alone!

Similarly, no isolated remarks about female silence in specific first- or second-century congregations can be used to undercut the grand and transparently clear biblical theme of believer priesthood. It was to all the Christians, women and men together, that Peter proclaimed, "You are a chosen generation, a royal priesthood, a holy nation" (1 Pet. 2:9). It was women and men together who were exhorted to offer up spiritual sacrifices (1 Pet. 2:5) and to "honor each other" (2:17), being "all of one mind" (3:8). It was to all the Christians at Corinth, to women and men together, that Paul wrote, "You may all prophesy one by one, that all may learn, and all may be comforted" (1 Cor. 14:31). It is only by assuming that the Bible is addressed to men only, with women's condition being addressed only in the passages that specify women, that a few difficult and culture-specific passages have been falsely utilized to render women secondary in the church and in society.

CULTURAL SPECIFICS CANNOT BE ABSOLUTIZED

I am not denying that the Bible contains many passages that reflect racist, sexist, classist, or heterosexist practices and customs. As we established earlier, the Bible is not a magic book. If God is the ultimate author of Scripture, God presumably could have spoken to human beings through a magic book; but clearly God chose instead to use human agents. As a consequence of that human agency, we readers must work hard to understand the cultural contexts through which the Bible was given to us.

Although much of the Bible reflects a time when kings ruled by divine right, we have not found it necessary to absolutize and cling to a monarchial form of government, let alone a monarchy by divine fiat. And although most of the Bible reflects a time when some human beings were enslaved by other human beings, the Bible establishes the full human worth of every human being, the fact that there is no favoritism with God, and the fact that in the New Creation, everybody is intended to respect and serve everybody else. Thus, we Christians do not take as normative those passages that reflect the cruel customs of slave-owning societies; rather, we take as normative the principles of human equality before God which are taught by the Hebrew prophets and the Christian Scriptures.

Furthermore, although all of the Bible was written during times when people assumed everybody to be naturally heterosexual, with homosexual behavior indulged in as an act of perverse lust or of pagan idolatry, it is time for the church to study the complexities of human sexuality and to learn about lifelong sexual orientations. It is time to lift up the theme of loving our neighbor as we love ourselves (the theme that is absolutely the *central* rule of the Judeo-Christian tradition) as normative over the few condemnations of homosexual abuses that occur in the Scriptures. There is no mention of homosexual love in Scripture unless we include, as interpreters did in the Middle Ages, the love of David and Jonathan and Ruth and Naomi. There is also no mention of the lifelong homosexual orientation in Scripture, because the understanding of sexual orientation did not develop until the late nineteenth century. When Scripture seems to be condemning homosexuals, it is actually condemning the loss of male sperm in a culture that needed population; or it is condemning pagan rituals, or prostitution, or exploitative lust, or the use of sex by some males to humiliate other males, as in the Sodom story. It is time for the heterosexuals in the church to love their homosexual neighbors as they love themselves, and to educate themselves about human sexuality so that they cease bearing false witness against their gay and lesbian neighbors.

At the time the Bible was written and also when many English Bible translations were made, handicapped people were often identified exclusively with their handicaps, so that people might be referred to simply as "lepers," "cripples," or "the deaf." Again, there is no reason to elevate the insensitivity of an earlier culture into a norm for the twentieth-century church. Because loving our neighbor as we love ourselves is absolutely basic to the Hebrew and Christian Scriptures, any customs and practices that we now understand to be unjust and unloving would violate that central norm of Judeo-Christian faith. We implement the basic biblical principle rather than the localized, culture-specific violations of it.

PATRIARCHAL LANGUAGE IN SCRIPTURE

During the times when the Bible was written, men held all the power in the family, in religion, and in society as a whole. Consequently, in order to honor God and affirm God's power, the biblical authors spoke of God primarily in masculine images—God as father, king, husband, and so forth. The really amazing thing is that here and there the biblical authors sometimes spoke of God in feminine images as well— God as mother, nurse, midwife, female householder, and so forth. That's amazing because it is not customary for a normative group to do so much honor to the group they regard as secondary to themselves. For the biblical authors to depict God as female in the midst of a patriarchal society is roughly analogous to a Ronald Reagan or Jeane Kirkpatrick speaking of God as a Communist! (Not that American conservatives are *oppressing* the Communists; but certainly they regard the Soviet Union as secondary to the United States, as the biblical authors inevitably regarded women as secondary to men.)

For me, it is one of the signs of inspiration from beyond themselves that the biblical authors were sometimes able to reach beyond their socialization to depict God as a woman. They also depicted God in nature images such as rock, vine, wind, living water, and so forth. Instead of clinging to the male images and masculine pronouns that have been used so exclusively that we have forgotten that God is not literally male, it is time for the church to expand upon the multiplicity of biblical images for God. Reassured by the fact that Jesus spoke of all three Persons of the Godhead in female images,[4] we may with confidence begin to alternate our use of male, female, and natural images for God, thus reminding ourselves that God is literally none of the above. And we may speak of God alternately with masculine pronouns, feminine pronouns, and neuter pronouns, thus breaking out of our idolatry and reminding ourselves that God's name is a verb: "I am who I am, " or "I am becoming who I am becoming." Again, in all of these areas of inclusiveness, I recommend study of the introduction and appendix to *An Inclusive Language Lectionary* as a short course in what it's all about.

THE NECESSITY AND THE PITFALLS OF BIBLE STUDY

I hope I have said enough to make clear why I think it was a dreadful error for mainline denominations to forget the Bible by underemphasizing serious Bible study. Although many Americans have never read much of the Bible, a great many would not want flagrantly to violate biblical principles. And if mainline-church people remain biblically illiterate, the Bible will be interpreted to the American public either by television evangelists, or by those who believe that the television evangelists' interpretations are the only interpretations, but dislike their message so much that they view the Bible as irrelevant and inimical to a righteous and decent human society. It is time for Christian churches to return to serious Bible study that pays attention to historical context and to the flow of ideas, images, and grammar within chapters and books and indeed pays attention to the whole overarching structure of the Hebrew and Christian Scriptures taken as a unit.

Such study is not without pitfalls. First, by definition, we must avoid the fundamentalist error of scorning the scholarship surrounding the Bible. Second, also by definition, we must also avoid the liberal error of assuming that modern people can "reach religious truth without learning humbly from God's self-revelation in the events and teachings recorded in the Bible."[5] Third, we must frankly recognize that no reader is objective: absolutely everyone reads through an interpretative grid, so that what counts as evidence for me may not count as evidence for you.[6] It is precisely because of this inevitable subjectivity that we literature professors try to teach our students (and ourselves) to pay painstaking attention to the surface of the text: word choice, sentence structure, imagery, analogy, spatial arrangement, literary type, and so forth. Only thus can we protect ourselves from sinking into such a miasma of eisogesis that we see only our own preconceived notions in whatever we read!

As always, the people who are most unconscious and naive about seeing through an interpretative grid are the ones who are most securely locked into it. What I call the grid, Paul called seeing "through a glass darkly," or seeing only a poor reflection in a dim mirror (1 Cor. 13:12). And his advice remains important: because knowledge will vanish away, it is vital never to violate love over differences of knowledge, which frequently (because of the grid) amount to differences of perception.

Acknowledging my own interpretative grid, I take as my central hermeneutical principle the "royal law" that was spoken by Moses and repeated by Jesus and again by Paul and again by James: "Thou shalt love thy neighbor as thyself." In my opinion, anything repeated word for word eight times in Scripture, and implied in hundreds of other passages, must qualify as the central hermeneutical norm by which all interpretations of all passages are judged. This book is an attempt to work out some of the implications of that "royal law" for everyday life, in a process I have called godding.

Because everyone has an interpretative grid, feminists engaged in serious Bible study must be on guard when they use Bible commentaries, study guides, and other scholarly tools, always allowing for the patriarchal assumptions that may have blinded the author to certain types of evidence. The works of Rosemary Ruether, Phyllis Trible, and Elisabeth Schussler-Fiorenza are particularly helpful in this regard. And I strongly recommend a 1985 book edited by Letty M. Russell, *Feminist Interpretation of the Bible.*

It is my hope that not only women but the whole church community will utilize as its central principle of interpretation the words of Jesus: "In everything, do to others what you would have them do to you, for this sums up the Law and the Prophets" (Matt. 7:12). It is another way of saying we should love our neighbors as we love ourselves. And since each of us wants the freedom of defining who we are and what we really want, that freedom is what we must give to one another.

SEEKING BALANCE

I have proposed the Bible as a kind of external check upon ego-inflation and narrowly selfish desires, but obviously the application of a literary text, however holy, is far from external. Because of our individual interpretative grids, with their inevitable limitations, we are all thrown back upon an "inner impulse." Like Samson, we may pay a very high price if we assume that because we were properly tuned to God's Spirit the last time, we are properly tuned this time as well. But there is no point in allowing the fear of error to paralyze us. From one perspective, at least, it is impossible to make a mistake; for as surely as the universe is "selving itself" within our experience, we can relax and simply fare forward.

Still, it is precisely because of our subjectivity that we are wise to reach toward whatever partial objectivity is available to us. (It is because I know that grading student work is a subjective process that I try to keep careful records and make my standards as clear and objective as I can). The knowledge that objectivity is a figment of patriarchal imaginations ought not to encourage us to wallow in subjectivity like pigs in slop, but rather to seek balance by measuring our impulses against accumulated human wisdom. For Christians and Jews, the Bible is basic to such wisdom.

Secular humanists, dismayed at the repressive uses to which the Bible has been put by people who do not read contextually, have suggested that we should forget about the Bible and construct entirely new myths that will foster racial, sexual, and economic justice. But Christian humanists are suggesting, and I agree, that instead of forgetting the Bible we confront it in a contextual and wholistic way. Although it inevitably reflects many of the harsh realities of the sexist, racist, and classist cultures in which the biblical authors lived, it is also alive with insight and significance. The roots of our Judeo-Christian tradition are biblical roots. While it is imperative that we grow into a more truly inclusive society, we will not grow by hacking away our roots.

NOTES

1. *Protestant Biblical Interpretation*, rev. ed. (Boston: W. A. Wilde Co., 1956), p. 17.

2. Quoted from a brochure of the Evangelical Women's Caucus International, 1357 Washington Street, Suite 5, West Newton, MA 02165.

3. "Woman, a Power Equal to Man," in *Biblical Archeological Review*, January-February 1983, pp. 56–68.

4. See Virginia Ramey Mollenkott, *The Divine Feminine* (New York: Crossroad, 1983). An incisive, brilliant discussion of inclusive language can be found in Sandra M. Schneiders, *Women and the Word* (New York: Paulist Press, 1986).

5. "Biblical Theology," in *The Harper Dictionary of Modern*

Thought, ed. Alan Bullock and Oliver Stallybrass (New York: Harper and Row, 1977).

6. An excellent study shows how the Bible has been interpreted through repressive and then liberating grids: Willard M. Swartley, *Slavery, Sabbath, War, and Women* (Scottdale, PA: Herald Press, 1983).

7

Peacemaking

In today's militaristic atmosphere, with nuclear stockpiles containing six thousand times more explosive power than was used in all of World War II, no activity of godding is quite as urgent as the work of peacemaking. Language has been so degraded in recent years by politicians who say one thing while they are doing another, that I hesitate even to use the word peacemaking. It brings to mind a tremendously destructive missile called the Peacekeeper! Yet the term peacemaking is not itself defiled; it is the misuse of the term that is defiled.

Every human being in the world "God so loved" is currently living under the threat of imminent holocaust. I use the word *holocaust* very deliberately, not in order to rob Jewish people of their history by transferring the Nazi outrage to a different context, but in order to indicate my instinctive reaction that the preparation and use of nuclear armaments is criminal and insane, *just* as criminally insane as Hitler's racist acts of genocide. I agree with Dorothee Soelle that nuclear bombs and missiles should not be dignified by calling them *weapons* "any more than the [Zyclon-B] gas of Auschwitz deserved to be called a 'weapon.'"[1] Like Zyclon-B gas, nuclear armaments are designed to destroy innocent human beings who are simply trying to live their lives in peace and have no idea of the anguish in store for them. Like the gas of Auschwitz, nuclear armaments deserve to be called *not* weapons of traditional warfare, as if they were aimed only at those involved in combat, but called what they really are: tools of mass destruction. As tools of mass destruction, nuclear armaments are a criminal outrage against human beings, who are made in the image of God. To stockpile tools of mass destruction is to prepare ourselves for another holocaust, this time on a worldwide scale. To stockpile tools of mass destruction is, quite literally, criminally insane. Nuclear armaments are illegal under international law,[2] and insane by any human standard.

USES OF THE BIBLE CONCERNING WAR

In chapter 6 I attempted a partial explanation of the importance of the Bible even in a culture where very few people actually read the Bible. On the issues of nuclear arms and warfare in general, the Bible has been used to legitimate policies that are deadly to humankind. And because people who love the world often have given up on the Bible, there are few voices making a cogent refutation.

Warfare has been biblically justified by pointing out that in the Hebrew Scriptures, there are more than thirty-five passages in which God ordered the use of armed force for carrying out divine purposes. The argument continues by insisting that God honored military leaders like Gideon and King David; and in the Christian Scriptures, Jesus commended the faith of a Roman centurion, and Peter was sent to speak to Cornelius, a soldier who is described as "God fearing," a man who "works righteousness." Jesus himself used physical force in cleansing the temple and violently denounced the enemies of God. The use of military imagery concerning the Christian experience, where the Christian is told to put on the whole armor of God (Eph. 6:10ff., 2 Tim. 2:3–4, Rev. 19:11,15), is taken to be a biblical endorsement of war. And when Jesus told people to pay their taxes (Matt.

17:27 and 22:21), that is also supposed to constitute an endorsement of war, since then as now a large percentage of the taxes would be devoted to paying for military activity. By the use of these arguments and others like them, people who respect the Bible have constructed the theory that under certain circumstances, war is not only justifiable but necessary. Today some people argue that nuclear holocaust was prophesied in the Bible as the destruction of the world by fire. Because the same people also believe that they themselves will have been caught up into heaven before the disaster occurs, they are noticeably unconcerned about the nuclear arms race, justifying it as a necessary deterrent to Soviet aggression.

USES OF THE BIBLE CONCERNING PEACE

Pacifists have used the Bible in a different way to arrive at a nonviolent ethic for biblical people. Instead of studying individual passages taken out of context, pacifists attempt to understand passages within their context—a more scholarly and productive way to study an issue. Although not all biblical pacifists would utilize the same arguments, we can discern a few major themes in their work. First, warfare is rooted in the alienation of humankind from God's creative intentions; hence, violence and warfare are sinful activities that ought to be overcome in the New Creation. Second, the Hebrew Scriptures do not glorify military deaths, nor do they develop war-hero stories like the Greek epics of Homer. Instead, the Hebrew Scriptures often criticize war, preparing for the New Testament teaching of nonviolence and pacifism. Such texts as Exodus 19 and 20 and Isaiah 2:1-4 teach that God's justice is established not by the sword, but by the Torah (the Word of God). The perspective of the Hebrew prophets is best summarized by Isaiah 30: 15: "In returning and rest you shall be saved; in quietness and in trust shall be your strength." In the world as we know it, "in trust shall be your strength" sounds almost like a foreign language! We Americans claim to trust God; but when we broadcast distrust of God's manifestations in human form, what does it mean to say that we trust God?

A third biblical pacifist theme is that the teachings of Jesus were clearly pacifist; he taught that evil should be overcome by goodness, not by more evil as a deterrent (Matt. 5:39–41). Fourth, the New Testament Epistles indicate that Christians are not to use evil means in the endeavor to "overcome evil with good" (Rom. 12:21; See also 1 Pet. 2:21–23; Phil. 2:5–11, 14–15). What could we term "evil means," if not stockpiles of nuclear armaments? When one bomb can release more firepower than all the explosives in all the wars in human history, even one is too many.

Fifth, as we saw in chapter 6, the central ethical norm in the Hebrew and Christian Scriptures is that we should love our neighbor as we love ourselves (Lev. 19:18; Matt. 19:19, 22:39; Mark 12:31; Luke 10:27; Rom. 13:9; Gal. 5:14; James 2:8). Because loving our neighbor is hardly compatible with *killing* our neighbor, this Judeo-Christian love-of-neighbor principle is considered by all pacifist thinkers to be the "moral muscle" of the biblical pacifist position.[3] The fact that Jesus instructed us to love even our *enemies* (Matt. 5:44), and that Jesus told one of his defenders to put away the sword even when it was used in self-defense (Matt. 26:52), only adds extra power to the Judeo-Christian principle that we are to love our neighbors as we love ourselves.

COLLAPSE OF THE "JUST WAR" THEORY

I have already distinguished between the weapons of conventional warfare and the nuclear tools of mass destruction that cannot properly be called weapons because they are intended to demolish innocent people in nonmilitary environments. I remind us of that distinction at this point because I believe that the "just war" theory cannot apply to nuclear warfare for that very reason. Until recently, *it was everywhere considered immoral to attack noncombatants*. America's napalming of Vietnamese women, children, and elderly people signaled an end of that kind of moral decency, as did the blitz bombings on both sides during World War II. But the atomic bombing of Hiroshima and Nagasaki constituted a new kind of horror. At the time of the bombing, the Japanese were already defeated and negotiating for peace. Furthermore, these two cities had not previously been bombed with conventional weapons and therefore were chosen to establish exactly what kind of damage atomic bombs could cause. Afterward, a special American hospital was set up to examine but not to treat the victims: it utilized the victims as guinea pigs in the scientific investigation of atomic-bomb damage.[4] The fact that the defeated Japanese were subjected to atomic bombs in order to give a clear postwar message not to their government but to the Soviet Union, constitutes a chilling use of human suffering for political purposes. Certainly it was a far cry from loving our Japanese neighbors as we love ourselves!

My point is that even if one *does* accept the argument that the Bible condones war under certain circumstances, this argument cannot apply to blitz bombing of nonmilitary targets and napalming of noncombatants, and certainly not to the use of nuclear tools of mass destruction! When it comes to nuclear warfare and other indiscriminate attack, *there can be no just war*. In the face of nuclear tools of mass destruction, biblical humanists, those concerned with godding, and all others who love the earth have no choice but to become nuclear pacifists.

INTERNATIONAL STEWARDSHIP

Because the mass media and rapid transportation have made the world a global village, it is imperative that we give up traditional notions of sovereignty and learn international cooperation in the stewardship of the world's resources—the food, oxygen, unpolluted water, and living space without which none of us can survive. As the nuclear accident at Chernobyl has recently illustrated, radioactivity does not respect national borders. So our concept of patriotism must assume a more global dimension than was necessary before the nuclear era.

The Second Vatican Council told us in 1965:

> Citizens should develop a generous and loyal devotion to their country, but without any narrowing of mind. In other words, they must always *look simultaneously to the welfare of the whole human family*, which is tied together by the manifold bonds linking races, peoples and nations.[5]

The idea of the entire human race as one family is, of course, a biblical idea; it received memorable expression in Saint Paul's sermon to the Greek philosophers on Mars Hill, as recorded in the seventeenth chapter of Acts. As I mentioned earlier, Paul said that God had made all nations of the earth from one single blood, and indeed Paul claimed that every human being lives, moves, and has being within the Being of God. Looked at from this biblical perspective, narrow loyalty to one nation as opposed to all other nations is disloyalty to the God who made and loves every single one of us. Divisions of the world into us versus them, however well they may have worked during the childhood of the human race, were always delusions and must now be given up if we are to survive.

Several decades ago psychologist R. D. Laing warned that "we are them to them as they are them to us," so that in the process of trying to get rid of *them*, we will also inevitably destroy *us*. And Jesus warned of something similar: "Whatever judgment you use on others is the same judgment by which you will be judged." As of now, the tools of mass destruction are in place. If we continue to live by nuclear armaments, we are going to die by nuclear armaments.

The nuclear holocaust could be started by an accident, a mere miscalculation, some irresponsible person tapping into the computers. Nuclear war almost happened in the early 1960s when a flock of geese set off a red alert on the early-warning radar system in Canada, and American bombers headed for Moscow and other Soviet cities. Fortunately the mistake was discovered in time and the bombers were recalled. Another close call occurred in November 1979, when a war-game tape was erroneously placed into the North American Air Defense computer system, and for six minutes jet fighters scrambled to intercept Soviet bombers and missiles that had been depicted as on their way to the United States. Just one minute before the president was to be notified so that he could decide whether to launch United States missiles, the error was detected! Later, in June 1980, two similar computer errors occurred.[6] Precious, beautiful, delicate life on Planet Earth hangs by a thread!

PEACEMAKING ACTIVITIES

What can we do? We can vote for candidates who will work for nuclear disarmament and the well-being of people everywhere. We can use all the media. We can try to help the people within our sphere of influence comprehend the folly of the arms race as a deterrent. If nuclear holocaust should occur, chances are good that it would be set off not by either of the two superpowers, but by some smaller nation heady with recently acquired nuclear power, or by a computer error, or by terrorist action. What, then, is the point of diverting funds that are desperately needed for food, lodging, health care, and other human services, into an ever escalating "balance" of superpower strike potential that is meaningless anyway? The world already contains more than forty-one thousand nuclear bombs and missiles. How much is enough?

Furthermore, we can gather the courage to insist upon gradual but determined progress toward nuclear disarmament—bilateral and verifiable if possible, but unilateral if necessary. Whatever danger unilateral disarmament would place us in could be no greater than the danger posed by the constant proliferation of instruments of mass destruction all over the world. As Lisa Peattie has written, with the descriptions of nuclear war that we now possess, we can be certain that "there is no conceivable national purpose for which the triggering of nuclear war would be sufficient justification." Furthermore, "the continuing institutionalized preparation for nuclear war brings us continually closer to the precipice of its occurrence." Therefore, we must move immediately to "eliminate preparation for nuclear war" and to stop an arms race that is gradually desensitizing us and "normalizing the unthinkable."[7]

In obedience to the biblical principle of truthfulness and clarity, and out of human decency, when we hear talk of a "preventative strike," we must translate that term into what it really means: a surprise attack. When we hear talk of "defense" or "security" we must recognize that these words have become euphemisms for the department of war. We must recognize the idolatry of naming warheads and missiles after mythological figures such as Poseidon, Trident, Jupiter, and Atlas, and placing our trust in them rather than in decent human negotiations. We must refuse to be lulled by language that refers to nuclear armaments as "gadgets," "cookie cutters," "Little Boy," "Peacekeeper," or "Honest John," or calms us with peaceful words like "*cruise* missile," "nuclear *exchange*,"[8] or "nuclear *umbrella*."

As for Star Wars—the president's Strategic Defense Initiative (SDI)—we could write to legislators and newspapers about the madness of building expensive and untestable instruments of mass destruction and then placing into space an expensive and untestable system that is supposed to *shield* us from what we human beings have built. The naiveté of the president's recent claim that the SDI system will protect us from attack just as a roof prevents rain from falling inside our houses would be touching if it were not so dangerous!

Other courses of action occurred to me after reading an article by William Broyles, Jr., the founding editor of *Texas Monthly* and a former editor of *Newsweek*. His article "Why Men Love War"[9] implicated traditional male socialization in militarism. Admitting that he enjoyed his tour of duty in Vietnam and had felt "bliss" at seeing dead Vietnamese loaded onto mechanical mules "like so much garbage," he wrote, "I had surrendered to an aesthetic that was divorced from that crucial quality of empathy that lets us feel the sufferings of others." If we train boys not to cry, not to express and preferably not even to feel their own sufferings, how can we expect them to grow into men who empathize with the sufferings of others? Broyles suggests to me that parents who "god" will carefully develop in their children the quality of empathy.

Broyles also makes a startling observation:

War may be the only way in which most men touch the mythic domains in our soul. It is, for some men, at some terrible level the closest thing to what childbirth is for women: the initiation into the power of life and death.

This suggests to my mind several peacemaking activities that might otherwise have seemed far removed from peacemaking: involving men more deeply in the birthing process; urging young men to get deeply involved in the arts and the humanities, where they will be put into contact with "the mythic domains" in the human soul; seeing that church services provide significant ritual rather than degenerating into mere "head trips"; and breaking our culture's barrier of isolation around dying people in order to provide mythic experience for all of us.

If we have the courage and the calling, we might also engage in nonviolent resistance against the United States military establishment. The Sojourners community in Washington, D.C., has an admirable record of such action, as do the Berrigan brothers and the Plowshares people and many others. Training in nonviolent resistance should precede such action; so should thinking through the penalties involved in civil disobedience.

THE VICTIMS OF THE NUCLEAR ARMS "RACE," THE RACE NOBODY CAN WIN

Every day, fifteen thousand people die because they have no food. Meanwhile governments worldwide are spending one million dollars a minute on nuclear armaments![10] Just a small percentage of what is being spent on the arms race could give all of the starving all the food they need. So these fifteen thousand people every day—mostly women and children because of the feminization of poverty[11]—are the casualties of the nuclear arms race. That's more than ten people a minute, dying for lack of food alone! Even if we never make active use of our instruments of mass destruction, already the casualties are mounting at the brutal pace of fifteen thousand innocent people every day. Meanwhile, domestic violence, violence against women and children, terrorism, and racial violence are all escalating. As we work toward nuclear disarmament, we need to keep in mind the biblical definition of peace as *shalom*, a definition that goes beyond the absence of war and even beyond the absence of overt violence to include the presence of justice. A peaceful world would be a world in which every member of every nation

> through nonviolent means, participates equally in a decisional power which regulates [the society] and the distribution of the resources which sustain it. Furthermore, a peaceful world would be a world in which no nation exploited or discriminated against any other nation.[12]

If we want peace, we must work for justice. The challenge is tremendous; but the alternative is assured mutual destruction, not merely as a policy but as a fact.

WE CANNOT SERVE GOD
AND NUCLEAR MILITARISM

According to my understanding of the Bible, it would be blasphemous to speak as though nuclear holocaust might be God's desire for the beautiful world that is God's handiwork. We cannot allow ourselves to dodge the fact that God gave to Adam and Eve responsibility for governing the world, symbolizing human responsibility for human society.

Faith in the God of the Bible is meaningful to the world only if that faith "helps to break our loyalties to less inclusive identities,"[13] such as our national, racial, religious, gender, or class identities. The God of the Bible is one God, and there is no favoritism with that one God. Hence we must conclude that God loves Libyans and Russians as much as Americans.

Because we live amid stockpiles of the tools of mass destruction, we can no longer serve God and militarism. Nobody's actions could be monstrous enough to justify the annihilation of the human race, so the just war theory is obsolete. We cannot remain silent while our governments prepare for the greatest crime in history, the murder and suicide of the human race, without becoming criminals ourselves. Either we will learn to love our neighbors as we love ourselves—including "the enemy" among our neighbors—or we will destroy ourselves in our attempts to destroy them. To paraphrase Ben Franklin, the nations of the earth must hang together or we will all hang separately, in one unholy holocaust.

People in the European peace movement have made a vow that is also a prayer. They have said, "Let there be disarmament, O God, and let it begin in Europe." My prayer and vow is this: "Let there be disarmament, O God, and let it begin in the United States."

NOTES

1. *The Arms Race Kills Even Without War* (Philadelphia: Fortress Press, 1983), p. 76.

2. "Lawyers Committee on Nuclear Policy, Statement on the Illegality of Nuclear Weapons," in *The Nuclear Predicament: A Sourcebook*, ed. Donna Athus Gregory (New York: St. Martin's Press, 1986), pp. 198–202.

3. For summaries of the just war and pacifist arguments along with clarification of the hermeneutical principles involved, see Willard M. Swartley, *Slavery, Sabbath, War, and Women* (Scottdale, PA: Herald Press, 1983), pp. 90–149.

4. Soelle, *The Arms Race Kills*, p. 99.

5. "Pastoral Constitution on the Church in the Modern World

(*Gaudium et Spes*)," no. 75. As quoted by Gerard A. Vanderhaar in *Christians and Nonviolence in the Nuclear Age: Scripture, the Arms Race, and You* (Mystic, CT: Twenty-Third Publications, 1982), p. 92. Emphasis mine.

6. Vanderhaar, *Christians and Nonviolence*, p.44.

7. "Normalizing the Unthinkable," in *The Nuclear Predicament*. This book is an excellent anthology of current opinions, including President Reagan's, and also provides historical documents that give readers a sense of how the dilemma developed.

8. See Paul Chilton, "Nukespeak: Nuclear Language, Culture, and Propaganda," in *The Nuclear Predicament*, pp. 127–42.

9. *Esquire*, November 1983. I have discussed this article at greater length in "Militarism: Exploring the Link between War and Sexism," in the Evangelical Women's Caucus *Update*, Sept. 1984–Feb. 1985, pp. 4–6.

10. *What About the Children?*, 5th printing (Moretown, VT: Parents and Teachers for Social Responsibility, 1984), p. 8. Copies of this powerful booklet are available for $1.00 each from PTSR, Box 517, Moretown, VT 05660.

11. On the interrelationship between systemic sexism and militarism, see Birgit Brock-Utne, *Educating for Peace: A Feminist Perspective* (New York: Pergamon Press, 1985).

12. Ibid., p. 2.

13. Gordon D. Kaufman, *Theology for a Nuclear Age* (Philadelphia: Westminster Press, 1985), p. 46. See also *Preaching on Peace*, ed. Ronald L. Sider and Darrel J. Brubaker (Philadelphia: Fortress Press, 1982).

8
Trusting the Whole Life Process

In chapter 6, I mentioned the importance of the accumulated wisdom of humankind as a somewhat "exterior" check to untrammeled egotism. Although that chapter focused on the Bible, accumulated human wisdom is also available in history, philosophy, and other literature, but nowhere more perfectly distilled than in poetry. I propose in this chapter to draw upon some of that wisdom.

Furthermore, in chapter 4, I explored the damage that has been done to Christian (and hence Western) experience by a focus on God as light, male, and warm to the exclusion of God as dark, female, and cold (materially embodied); and we examined some of the positive images of darkness and negative images of light that are available to us in biblical literature. In this chapter I plan to build on the dark-light polarity (the necessary tension or alternation between darkness and light) as I examine in poetry the theme of opposites generating each other. Continuing a theme introduced in chapter 2, I hope also to build on the understanding of God as all-encompassing Reality, as we saw in the Book of Job, all the while pondering this question: How can a loving God, the God of the Bible, encompass matter as well as spirit, dark as well as light, female as well as male, "bad" as well as good? I am not so foolish as to attempt a definitive definition of the nature of God, but will simply attempt to be honest about how God seems to be, from the empirical human perspective.

POLARITIES OF THE WEST AND EAST

In his book *Opposition*,[1] C. K. Ogden has shown that Aristotle regarded everything as proceeding from contraries. Ogden also shows the importance of opposition in the philosophies of people like Jacob Boehme, Immanuel Kant, and Frederick Hegel. Similarly, Heraclitus emphasized the constant equality of opposites in conflict, using the term *enantiodromia* to describe the law of opposites flowing constantly into each other. The followers of Pythagoras specified certain sets of opposites as the major oppositions through which the world is to be understood. Among the Pythagorean opposites are limit and unlimit, odd and even, one and many, right and left, male and female, rest and motion, straight and curved, light and dark, and good and bad.

Eastern religions like Taoism, Confucianism, Buddhism, and some forms of Hinduism also stress the constant flow of opposites into one another. Anyone who has worked with the *I Ching*,[2] the Taoist Book of Changes, is well aware of the principle that when something grows extremely yang, it is about to change into yin, and when something grows exceedingly yin, it is on the verge of transformation into yang. Because yin is the receptive, so-called "feminine," unconscious, dark principle, and yang is the assertive, "masculine," conscious, light principle, we could also say that the *I Ching* works according to the dynamic that when something becomes too light, it is about to change into darkness, and when it becomes too dark, it is about to change into light.

If these religions have any truth in them, then surely Christian theology has harmed people by asking them to live exclusively in the light, in total repudiation of darkness. I am of course aware that the First Epistle of John makes the claim that "God is light, and in [God] is no darkness at all" (1:5). The context indicates that for John, God is the Source of light, which John uses as a metaphor for love and knowledge. To John, people who hate their sisters and brothers are in darkness (2:11). I do not deny the validity of John's metaphors within his own context; I simply suggest that we need to reflect the whole range of biblical metaphors and images, rather than a single set of metaphors that legitimate the concepts we are used to, the ones we find politically convenient.

Algernon Swinburne's sneering verses, although inaccurate concerning the vitality of Jesus, do contain some truth when applied to traditional Christian adulation of light and repudiation of darkness, since denial of opposites leads to a bland deadness. Swinburne wrote, "Thou hast conquered, O pale Galilean/The world has grown grey from thy breath."[3] From this perspective the traditional Catholic prayer for the dead, "May perpetual light shine upon them," sounds more like the gruelling and stultifying spotlight of a police lineup than like fertile and relaxed blessedness!

MILTON'S IMAGINATIVE EMBODIMENT OF CONTRARIES

What great philosophers have made explicit, great artists have rendered in images. In *Paradise Lost*, Milton speaks of God's robes as being "Dark with excessive bright," a perfect image of *enantiodromia*, or opposites flowing into one another. According to Milton's image, the robes of God are so brilliant that they bedazzle heaven and force even the seraphim to veil their eyes with both their wings: "Dark with excessive bright thy skirts appear."[4]

It is not only in this one image that Milton intuits the constant and necessary interaction of opposites within a universe that is encompassed by the nature of God. To Milton, God's nature "contains both the Deep and its coincident Night."[5]

In *Paradise Lost* Milton's God asserts that the Deep is bound-less precisely because "I am who fill/ Infinitude, nor vacuous the space . . ." (bk. 7, lines 168–69). This means that Milton's God fills darkness as well as light, indeed *is* darkness as well as light.

If we step back from *Paradise Lost* to look at its whole structure, including its unconscious meanings, we could eas-ily see Milton's Satan as a dark split-off from God's own mind, much as the Book of Job suggests that the Adversary or Satan is a shadow of God's own nature. For everything that occurs in heaven, there is a parallel occurrence in hell—a mirror image—except that in hell the motive is to destroy rather than to save. For instance, just as Milton's heaven contains a trinity of Father, Son, and (in a very derivative role) the Spirit or Muse, hell also has its trinity: Satan; Sin, the daughter who springs full-grown from his brain, whom he marries; and the child of their incestuous union, Death. Ponder the insight that could be obtained by reading the Christian trinity in the light of Milton's parody! Milton no doubt drew the sex and birthing images of his demonic trinity from James 1:15: "When lust has conceived, it brings forth sin; and sin, when it is finished, brings forth death." Now if, as the creeds suggest, the Holy Spirit proceeds from the Father and the Son, then the Son is symbolically both God's daughter and God's wife—and Dame Julian of Norwich's vision of Christ as Mother is not so unusual an image after all! I am not asking that we become heavily literal about these matters; but surely we have trun-cated our own humanity by failing to include a dark or female or unconscious dimension in our understanding of the divine nature!

Milton is positively brilliant in his description of the inter-action of good and evil in a fallen world:

> Good and evil we know in the field of this world grow up
> almost inseparably; and the knowledge of good is so involved

and interwoven with the knowledge of evil, and in so many cunning resemblances hardly to be discerned, that those confused seeds which were imposed upon Psyche as an incessant labor to cull out and sort asunder, were not more intermixed. It was from out the rind of one apple tasted that the knowledge of good and evil, as two twins cleaving together, leaped forth into the world. And perhaps this is that doom which Adam fell into of knowing good *and* evil, that is to say, of knowing good *by* evil.[6]

Let's be sure we grasp the implications of Milton's imagery. He alludes to the classical myth of Psyche, who angered Venus by winning the love of Cupid. Venus doomed Psyche to sorting out the various kinds of grain from a tremendous heap of intermingled grains, and Psyche would be at it still had not the ants taken pity upon her and organized themselves to do the work for her. What an image of the way personal hangups and complexes provide the impetus for our minds to work their way toward wholeness! What Psyche could not possibly do alone, the lowly ants working together accomplished for her. Milton also describes good and evil as inseparable Siamese twins; to attempt to part them would be to kill them both. And he interprets the story of the Tree of the Knowledge of Good and Evil to mean that once Adam and Eve have eaten of it, they will never again know good by itself, but will know good only by opposition or contrast to evil. Thus, to spend time picking through our motives, judging our feelings and trying to eliminate all "darkness" from our personalities, would be worse than useless: it would be positively destructive of the creative and powerful goodness that arises in tension or interaction with what we tend to call "evil" or "bad" or "negative" or "dark."

I am astonished that of all the sermons I have heard in my fifty-five years, I have never heard a preacher utilizing any of these Miltonic insights and images. Although Milton makes clear that his Muse is to be identified as the Spirit of God the

Father, he several times addresses that Spirit as female, and confesses that She brings his inspiration to him at night, so that his poetry is "easy" and "involuntary."[7] His poetry, Milton says, is actually "Hers, who brings it nightly to mine ear." Milton confesses that without the Muse who comes to him in the double darkness of blindness and night, his inspiration would dry up. Hence, the many passionate invocations of the Muse in Milton's poetry reveal that Milton's "genius (like that of all great minds) lay in the power to stay close to the unconscious."[8] And the unconscious is, of course, "female" and "dark." Those of us who are too busy to interpret and learn from our dreams may accurately describe ourselves as entirely too busy!

Milton also made clear that after he had gone blind in midlife, God compensated him with inward eyes and special insight. Thus he placed himself in the Homeric tradition of the blind prophet who sees more clearly in darkness than most others do in the light.

Milton asserted that Adam and Eve transmitted to their children not only bodies, but also a human psyche, a racial soul that is analogous to Jung's concept of a collective unconscious.[9] If any readers have thought of Milton as a rigid and puritanical fuddy-duddy, I suggest they lay aside that notion and return to his work. It is particularly helpful when read as psychodrama for the insights it can offer concerning the struggle toward human wholeness. And such *beauty!*

MARIANNE MOORE ON CONTRARIES

It should come as no surprise that women who write poetry are often attracted to the *enantiodromia* theme of opposites flowing into each other. Modern American poet Marianne Moore offers her particular insight in a poem entitled "Sojourn in the Whale." Addressed to Ireland, victim of numerous famines and of exploitation by England, the poem admires Ireland's "female," waterlike adaptability and unstoppability:

> Trying to open locked doors with a sword, threading
>   the points of needles, planting shade trees
>   upside down; swallowed by the opaqueness of one whom
> the seas
>
> love better than they love you, Ireland—
> you have lived and lived on every kind of shortage.
>   you have been compelled by hags to spin
>   gold thread from straw[10] and have heard men say;
> "There is a feminine temperament in direct contrast to
> ours
>
> Which makes her do these things. Circumscribed by a
>   heritage of blindness and native
>   incompetence, she will become wise and will be
>   forced to give in.
> Compelled by experience, she will turn back;
> Water seeks its own level":
>   and you [Ireland] have smiled. "Water in motion is
>   far from level." You have seen it, when obstacles
>   happened
>   to bar
>   the path, rise automatically.

The only allusion to Jonah in the poem occurs in the title, "Sojourn in the Whale." Ireland's oppressed condition is implicitly compared to the helpless condition of Jonah in the darkness of the whale's belly, forced by circumstances simply to wait. Ireland is also compared to a woman in sexist society, a woman whom male oppressors define as natively incompetent, possessor of a loser's temperament totally different from their own. Thus Moore implies the reason for the human tendency to split our consciousness away from other people by placing them in categories other than our own. If we can only convince ourselves that others do not feel things the same way we ourselves feel them, that their temperament is in direct contrast to ours, then we can exploit or reject others with confidence and without guilt.

But Ireland, symbolizing both oppressed people everywhere and the repressed or oppressed aspects of our own beings, *smiles* when she is compared to water. "Water seeks its own level" is a cliché that implies downward mobility. But Ireland smiles because she knows that in fact "Water in motion is far from level." When obstacles happen to bar the path of water in motion, the water rises automatically; the obstacle is the instigator or trigger of the successful adaptation of the water, the automatic rising of it. The more formidable the obstacle, the greater the rising. Difficulty becomes opportunity becomes transcendence becomes new difficulty. . . .

PERSONAL EXPERIENCE:
THE POWER OF OPPOSITIONS

Not long ago, feeling very afraid of my own inner process, I tried to circumvent my conscious mind and to get in touch with my deeper awareness by asking the *I Ching* what attitude I should take in my current difficulties. The hexagram I received was number twenty-nine, the Abysmal (Water). The image central to this hexagram is that of a person in danger, "like water in the depths of an abyss or ravine. The water shows [me] how to behave: it flows on without piling up anywhere, and even in dangerous places it does not lose its dependable character. In this way the danger is overcome."[11] I took this to mean that I should stop judging myself for being in the ravine and simply flow forward like water, receptive to the changing circumstances (the sides of the ravine) and learning whatever my difficult surroundings might have to teach me, relinquishing my yang desire to understand and control everything in the light, learning instead to relax into a more yin acceptance of mystery and surprise in the dark abyss. Like Marianne Moore's Ireland, I have begun to learn that within my own Christian life experience, "Water in motion is far/from level. [I] have seen it, when obstacles happened/to bar/the path, rise automatically." Difficult external circumstances and terrifying internal realities have for me flowed into their opposite, into a rising of strength that I would not have believed before, putting me in touch with whole new dimensions of myself and allowing me to change old patterns that are no longer appropriate for me.

This fairly recent understanding of reality comes as a tremendous relief after my former striving for a rigid perfection, a Christlikeness that was all sweetness and light and definitely not me. Not Christ either, probably! The notion of imitating Christ would not have been so pernicious had we constantly paid attention to the *enantiodromia* Jesus' life displayed. Like the rest of us, he "learned obedience by the things he *suffered*" (Heb. 5:8). Why then have we Christians been taught to feel guilty about our sufferings, depressions, and griefs? Jesus' words about being perfect (Matt. 5:48) have caused mental torment whenever they have been interpreted as meaning perfect contentment and happiness at all times. How much healthier we Christians would be were we persuaded from every pulpit in the land that Jesus was telling us to be complete, to be whole, as our Mother and Father in heaven is complete and whole! (*Teleios*, translated as "perfect" in the King James Version of Matthew 5:48, means "complete.") Such an emphasis would help us embrace our psychological process in its entirety, the darkness as well as the brightness, the ebb as well as the flow, the yin and the yang together.

AUDRE LORDE ON THE BLACK MATRIX

Contemporary poet Audre Lorde writes of a different kind of *enantiodromia*, the brilliance that flashes out of blackness. Describing herself as a "black lesbian feminist warrior poet," Lorde writes about the erotic as "the deepest life force, a force which moves us toward living in a fundamental way." When she speaks of living, she explains, she means "the force which moves us toward what will accomplish real positive change."[12]

Just as Genesis provides us with the image of a dark abyss from which God differentiated darkness and light and then synthesized them into a single polar unit, Audre Lorde's poem titled "Coal" provides a marvelous image of blackness as the matrix of diamondlike brilliance:

> I
> is the total black, being spoken
> from the earth's inside.
> There are many kinds of *open*
> how a diamond comes into a knot of flame
> how sound comes into a word, colored
> by who pays what for speaking.
>
> Some words are open like a diamond
> on glass windows
> singing out within the passing crash of sun
> Then there are words like stapled wagers
> in a perforated book,—buy and sign and tear apart—
> and come whatever wills, all chances,
> the stub remains
> and ill-pulled tooth with a ragged edge.
>
> Some words live in my throat
> breeding like adders. Others know sun
> seeking like gypsies over my tongue

to explode through my lips
like young sparrows bursting from shell
Some words
bedevil me.

Love is a word, another kind of open.
As the diamond comes into a knot of flame
I am Black because I come from the earth's inside
now take my word for jewel in the open light.[13]

Here Audre Lorde comments on words and the many different levels of reality words can come from. The most truthful words are the "blackest," those that come up from the depths of anyone's personal earth. Like coal that is black because it comes from the earth's inside, real Love is black, and when spoken becomes a knot of flame in the open light. Here there is no denial of body, of darkness, of matter, or of sexuality, including female sexuality. In my opinion, Christianity needs more *coal*, more of what comes "from the earth's inside." We have not yet cured ourselves of the too-bright imbalances of Greek antiphysical emphases.

ADRIENNE RICH CRITIQUES PATRIARCHY'S ONE-WAY ENERGY

Another distinguished lesbian feminist poet, Adrienne Rich, says some things about male poets that apply to many traditional Christians as well. It is a long quotation, but well worth our attention.

Rich commented in 1971:

To the eyes of a feminist, the work of Western male poets now writing reveals a deep, fatalistic pessimism as to the *possibilities of change* whether societal or personal, along

with a familiar and threadbare use of women (and nature) as
redemptive on the one hand, threatening on the other, and a
new rise of phallocentric sadism and overt woman-hating
which matches the sexual brutality of recent films. Political
poetry by men remains stranded amid the struggles for power
among male groups; in condemning U.S. materialism or the
Chilean junta the poet can claim to speak for the oppressed
while remaining, as male, part of a system of sexual oppression. The enemy is always outside the self, the struggle some-
where else. The mood of isolation, self-pity, and self-imitation
that pervades 'nonpolitical' poetry suggests that a profound
change in masculine consciousness will have to precede any
new male poetic—or other—inspiration. The creative energy
of patriarchy is fast running out; what remains is its self-
generating energy for destruction. As women, we have our
work cut out for us.[14]

I would amend Adrienne Rich's final statement to say that
we feminist women and men who are willing to include in
our Christianity the positive aspects of darkness—the positive
aspects of matter, of women, of mystery, of tentativeness, of
our own suffering, and even in a sense the positive aspects of
"evil" as a necessary part of the human process—we women
and men together have our work cut out for us. The creative
energy of patriarchy is indeed fast running out and is trying to
shore itself up with nuclear bombs and missiles. The opposite
of patriarchy is not matriarchy, but mutuality—and therein
lies our hope.

IS SIN NECESSARY?

I would like to clarify that I recognize evil as a force to
struggle against tirelessly *if* we are speaking about personal
alienation or about the oppressive systems of racism, sexism,

classism, heterosexism, and the like. Yet if we are to have any inner peace and joy, we must combat social injustice in the spirit taught by Jesus to Dame Julian of Norwich at a time when she was upset about the problem of evil. Jesus said to her: "Sin is necessary: but all will be well, and all will be well, and every kind of thing will be well."[15] That is, we must work for justice and peace with a constant *dual* awareness: an awareness that in the temporal dimension, injustice is an evil that must be overcome, but with a simultaneous awareness that in the eternal dimension, injustice is already overcome and we are actors in a divine comedy.

Perhaps an illustration drawn from the field of parapsychology will clarify what I am talking about. Laurence Le Shan explains that clairvoyants, when they are in the special relationship to reality in which they are able to use their extrasensory perceptions, simply observe and do not judge. They are so aware of a universal space-time fabric of being that "to judge any specific event as good or evil is to judge the entire cosmos." On the ordinary sensory level of reality, however, they would not deny that pain, disease, alienation, and deprivation are evil and should be avoided if possible.[16] We saw this dual awareness in the Book of Job, in the calmness of the Prologue and Epilogue as opposed to the human distress of the poetry that forms most of the book.

ANOTHER WAY OF LOOKING AT THINGS

Awareness of the eternal dimension has the effect of encouraging "godders" in the face of constant setbacks on the temporal plane. Rather than robbing us of our stamina and determination, the simultaneous awareness of another dimension preserves us from burnout (provided we attend to it often enough). In one sense, it is this dual awareness that is symbolized by the theme we have been examining, the *enantiodromia* theme of opposites flowing into one another during the process of temporal reality as we know it.

In my opinion, traditional Christianity has taken what the Bible says about the eternal perspective (the whole field or process of reality seen simultaneously and wholistically) and has imposed it on the limited temporal perspective like a Procrustean bed that simply lops off whatever realities don't fit the theory.

As T. S. Eliot remarked, most overtly Christian poetry is dreadful because people write about what they wish they felt rather than what they actually do feel. But the great poets, including Eliot himself, write about what the human condition truly feels like: and what it feels like is a constant *enantiodromia* in which the darkness and light within individuals and within the human race flow into each other as constantly as day and night flow into each other. The only way we can avoid the despair of Sisyphus pushing his ever-returning rock up the mountain is to keep our minds aware of that "other country" while we do what needs to be done in this one. In the other country of the constant present tense, salvation is simultaneously beginning, proceeding, and perfected; wholeness is a process that all at once is commencing, growing, and accomplished. But in this realm where we are trapped in a constant succession of moments flowing from future to past, there never fails to be more work to be done.

What I have been suggesting throughout this book is that our faith will be far healthier when we are more fully, honestly, and authentically human; that our Christian attempt to walk constantly in the light stems from focus on certain Scriptural images to the exclusion of certain other images, and causes a truncation of our humanity; and that our movement toward wholeness may be assisted by closer attention to the experience crafted for us not only by life itself, but by our greatest writers. Too often we have lived like Job's friends, attempting to cram human experience into the mold of our doctrines and theories instead of telling the truth about what life seems to have taught us.

Great artists give us vicarious experience of what life has taught to them. For instance, in his masterpiece *Troilus and Criseyde*, Geoffrey Chaucer describes Troilus's elation when he wins Criseyde's love and his agony when he is deserted by her and then is killed in battle. But after death, Troilus is caught up into the eighth sphere and looks down at "this little spot of earth" and at those who are weeping over his death. And he laughs! Job, too, must have laughed if and when he found out that he had suffered as God's champion. If only we could learn to flow with life's vicissitudes (its *enantiodromia*) with a remembrance of that other, larger dimension! But perhaps our forgetfulness of it is precisely part of the condition of being human; certainly judging ourselves for our forgetfulness is worse than useless. Fare forward!

WRESTLING WITH GOD, WRESTLING AS GOD

A sonnet by Jesuit poet Gerard Manley Hopkins illustrates several of the points I have been trying to make about the human responsibility of godding. The speaker in the sonnet is in the midst of terrible personal suffering. He cries out in Job-like anger at the cruelty God seems to be manifesting. Behind the sonnet lies the story told in Genesis 32:24–30 of Jacob wrestling with Someone all through the darkness of the night, a marvelous image of our struggles toward wholeness. Only when morning came did Jacob recognize that the One who both blessed and crippled him had been none other than God's Very Self. Hopkins' speaker asks himself why he is undergoing so much suffering, and makes the creative response that he is being made more truly authentic by the suffering—that his chaff (his distorted response to reality) is being threshed away to leave the grain of his authentic core lying "sheer and clear." He wonders for whom he is cheering during the wrestling match: for the hero-wrestler from heaven, or for himself; and like Job, he realizes that to cheer for the heavenly wrestler is also to cheer for himself, and to cheer for himself is to cheer for the heavenly wrestler. They are not separate after all, but flowing into and completing each other. Wrestling is in fact an excellent image of *enantiodromia*, because once the wrestlers are locked together, it is hard to tell where one person stops and the other begins. In this case, the *enantiodromia* is between God and a human being. Is God in Jacob or is Jacob in God? Both.

Out of the agony of that dark night's wrestling comes the epiphany; and the speaker catches his breath with the awesome recognition of Who It Is who has bruised and blessed him. Here is the sonnet, untitled by Hopkins but called "Carrion Comfort" by Robert Bridges in the 1918 edition:

> Not, I'll not, carrion comfort, Despair, not feast
>   on thee,
> Not untwist—slack they may be—these last
>   strands of man
> In me or, most weary, cry I can no more. I can;
> Can something, hope, wish day come, not choose
>   not to be.
> But ah, oh thou terrible, why wouldst thou
>   rude on me
> Thy wring-world right foot rock? lay a
>   lionlimb against me? scan
> With darksome devouring eyes my bruised
>   bones? and fan,
> O in turns of tempest, me heaped there; me
>   frantic to avoid thee and flee?
> Why? That my chaff might fly; my grain
>   lie, sheer and clear.

Nay, in all that toil, that coil, since (seems)
    I kissed the rod,
Hand rather, my heart lo! lapped strength, stole
    joy, would laugh, cheer.
Cheer whom though? the hero whose heaven-handling
    flung me, foot trod
Me? Or me that fought him? O which one? is
    it each one? That night, that year
Of now done darkness I wretch lay wrestling
    with (my God!) my God.

There is no label on the person who rudely, abruptly takes hold of Jacob to wrestle in the darkness, no sign to tell Jacob that this truly awful and terrifying experience is an experience of God. And nobody ever tells Job what had happened during the Prologue behind the scenes in heaven; so he never knew during his earthly experience that he had suffered as God's champion. Nobody ever told Hopkins that the inner anguish out of which he wrote the "terrible sonnets" was a divine process within him that ultimately would bring help to thousands of others because Hopkins, godding, managed the *enantiodromia* of transforming his pain into beauty. (Even the experience of reading Hopkins's work is an experience of *enantiodromia*: at first a poem seems snarled and almost meaningless. But on the fourth or fifth reading it suddenly explodes into meaning and beauty).

EVERYDAY EPIPHANIES

Like Job, like Jacob, human beings are rarely told that our suffering is part of a universal struggle toward wholeness. In fact, for many of us, a central aspect of our agony is that our training tells us that our suffering must certainly stem from our own wrongness. Somehow, we must deserve it.

But Jacob hangs on to the unknown opponent until he wins a blessing. And Job sticks to his own experience of reality until his honesty brings him a larger vision. In his personal darkness Milton's divine woman enables him to see a God who is "dark with excessive bright." Audrey Lorde proudly speaks about flashing diamond love out of the matrix of coal-blackness. And Marianne Moore's Ireland rises like an ocean wave encountering the rocky walls of a ravine. As with all of them, if the rest of us hope to know God here and now, the encounter will have to happen within the *enantiodromia*— the changefulness, the pressures, and the material embodi-ment—of our own experiences and our own moods. We would be wise to cease judging our experience, cease repressing our "shadow selves," cease attempting to force ourselves into always-happiness and always-rationality and always-busy-ness. Things will no doubt be different when the whole universe has achieved "the glory which shall be revealed" (Rom. 8: 18–23). But meanwhile, if we hope to enjoy light, we'd better not deny the darkness that is its context.

NOTES

1. (Bloomington: Indiana University Press, 1932; reprinted, 1967).

2. The most scholarly edition of the *I Ching* in English is the Richard Wilhelm Translation Rendered into English by Cary F. Baynes, with a Foreword by C. G. Jung, Bollingen Series 19 (Princeton University Press, 1950). A good paperback edition is edited by Sam Reiffer (New York: Bantam, 1974).

3. "Hymn to Proserpine" (1866).

4. *Paradise Lost*, bk. 3, line 380.

5. "Metaphysics," *A Milton Encyclopedia*, Vol.5 (Lewisburg, PA: Bucknell University Press, 1979).

6. *Areopagitica* (1644).

7. See Virginia R. Mollenkott, "Some Implications of Milton's Androgynous Muse," in *Bucknell Review: Women, Literature, and Cricitism*, 24 (Spring 1978), pp. 27–36.

8. "Psychology and Milton," in *A Milton Encyclopedia*, Vol. 7.

9. "Christian Doctrine," in *The Works of John Milton*, Vol. 15 (New York: Columbia University Press), pp. 39–53.

10. Moore alludes to the folktale "Rumplestiltskin," in which a maiden is forced by a king to spin straw into gold. "Sojourn in the Whale" and hundreds of other works by women are available in Sandra M. Gilbert and Susan Gubar, eds., *The Norton Anthology of Literature by Women: The Tradition in English* (New York: W. W. Norton, 1985). "Sojourn in the Whale" appears on pp. 1493-94.

11. *The I Ching*, Bollingen Series 19, p. 532.

12. As quoted by Gilbert and Gubar, in *The Norton Anthology of Literature by Women*, p. 2250.

13. *The Norton Anthology of Literature by Women*, p. 2250.

14. "When We Dead Awaken: Writing as Re-Vision (1971)," in *The Norton Anthology of Literature by Women*, p. 2056.

15. Julian of Norwich, *Showings*, translated and introduced by Edmund Colledge, O.S.A., and James Walsh, S.J. (New York: Paulist Press, 1978), p.225.

16. *The Medium, the Mystic, and the Physicist* (New York: Balantine Books, 1966), p. 38.

9

No Coward Soul Is Ours

In January 1846, at the age of twenty-eight and just two years before her death, Emily Brontë wrote these lines:

> No coward soul is mine,
> No trembler in the world's storm-troubled sphere;
> I see Heaven's glories shine
> And Faith shines equal, arming me from Fear.
>
> O God within my breast
> Almighty ever-present Deity
> Life, that in me hast rest,
> As I, Undying Life, have power in Thee:
>
> Vain are the thousand creeds
> That move men's hearts, unutterably vain,
> Worthless as withered weeds
> Or idlest froth amid the boundless main
>
> To waken doubt in one
> Holding so fast by thy infinity,
> So surely anchored on
> The steadfast rock of Immortality.
>
> With wide embracing love
> Thy spirit animates eternal years,
> Pervades and broods above,
> Changes, sustains, dissolves, creates, and rears.

> Though earth and moon were gone
> And suns and universes ceased to be
> And thou wert left alone
> Every Existence would exist in Thee.
>
> There is no room for Death,
> Nor atom that his might could render void,
> Since thou art Being and Breath—
> And what thou art may never be destroyed.[1]

Is this pantheism? Does it identify God with the natural creation? Certainly not, for although Brontë addresses God within herself, she recognizes that earth, moon, suns, and universes are dependent on God's being, but not the other way around. Pan*en*theism it may be, for Brontë asserts that everything exists *in* God and God *in* everything, yet she does not limit God to the human process or even the universal process.

There is transcendence, for God "broods above," "creates" in "infinity," and is "Undying Life." There is immanence, for God "pervades" and "changes, sustains, dissolves, and rears," and lives within the human breast. If Brontë is pan-entheistic, she has plenty of biblical precedent for being so: Ephesians 4:6 describes the one God, who is Father and Mother to us all, as being "*above* all and *through* all and *in* all," and there are other passages that say similar things (see the Appendix).

Interestingly enough, Brontë, who was the daughter of a Yorkshire clergyman, saw creeds as vain—not because they could not *foster* faith, but because they could not *destroy* faith! Apparently it never even occurred to her to think that creeds could help to make faith happen! But she knew from experience that creeds could certainly erode peace by awakening doubt in people who were anchored on something less solid than their own experience of "the steadfast rock of Immortality." For those like herself who hold firmly to a conviction of God's indestructible infinity, creeds are as worthless as weeds or bubbles on the open ocean.

EMILY BRONTË'S MYSTICISM

Is Emily Brontë self-intoxicated when she claims that God Almighty is within her, that indeed her soul is one with God, and that her courage and her power originate from her being in God? (Stanza two tells us that "Deity/Life" has found "rest" in her body-self, while her body-self derives its power from "Undying Life.") I certainly cannot believe that Brontë's claim is inflated: on the contrary, she is making the claim that mystics of every religion and mystics of no religion have always made. And it is a biblical claim, implicit in the Hebrew Scriptures and quite explicit in the Christian Scriptures (see the Appendix for further details, especially regarding 1 John 4:12–13).

Brontë is talking about godding. Because her soul is not limited to her frail little body (her coffin was only five and a half feet long and sixteen inches wide), she is able to live undaunted in "the storm-troubled sphere" of this world. During her short life she gave the world one of its most powerful novels of passion, vengeance, and redemption, *Wuthering Heights* (1847). She also nursed her brother, Branwell, during his final days, after he had become addicted to alcohol and opium. So self-disciplined was this woman that she resolutely went about her business during the final two months of her fatal illness, getting out of bed and dressing herself even on the day she died.

MYSTICISM AND THE CHRISTIAN COMMUNITY

Emily Brontë's type of mysticism and godding well illustrates what has made the Christian church nervous about mystics through the ages, and what makes the modern church nervous about Christian feminist "godders." Her swift dismissal of creeds is typical of mystics. Having had a firsthand experience of God within, what need did she have for all that creedal codification of belief? Faith goes much deeper than mere belief!

Mystics also tend to be impatient with any human authority over them. Having seen "Heaven's glories shine," and knowing that Faith shines just as brightly as Heaven in order to arm her against Fear, Emily Brontë does not need anyone to mediate God's will to her. In a poem published posthumously by her sister Charlotte Brontë, Emily says, "I'll walk where my own nature would be leading/It vexes me to choose another guide."[2] She can say this without selfish egotism because she knows her connectedness to the Undying Life of all creatures. Still, there is about her an ungovernability that is to some degree typical of mystics and that threatens to undermine church hierarchies.

EMILY BRONTË'S FEMINISM

In that posthumous poem Emily Brontë makes clear that nothing she has written about the infinity of spirit is to be construed as dismissing the importance of nature. The Undying Life *needs* human embodiment to "rest" in; and she expands "my own nature" to mean not simply the personality and body-self named Emily Brontë, but the whole natural process in which everything worthwhile can be learned:

> I'll walk where my own nature would be leading:
> It vexes me to choose another guide:
> Where the gray flocks in ferny glens are feeding;
> Where the wild wind blows on the mountainside.
>
> What have these lovely mountains worth revealing?
> More glory and more grief than I can tell:

> The earth that wakes one human heart to feeling
> Can centre both the worlds of Heaven and Hell.

Here is the insistence on concrete this-worldliness that contemporary feminism also manifests. Here also is the emphasis on trusting one's own experience rather than relying on dogma doled out by priests who sometimes resemble Job's friends.

When the Brontës were growing up, Emily and Anne developed an imaginary country named Gondal and wrote the chronicles of that land. Significantly, it was governed by a powerful queen whom Emily sometimes referred to as "Sidonia's *deity*." Since she remained committed to Gondal and Gondal's queenly deity well past her teenage years, we know that Emily Brontë's imagination took her far beyond the all-male godhead she learned about in her father's parsonage. It is significant that she refers to God in gender-neutral terminology and assigns to nature a primacy in teaching human beings how to *feel*. Brontë's is "no coward soul" because imaginatively she was able to claim her identity with a female deity and with the power of nature.

CONSCIOUS AND UNCONSCIOUS WORSHIP IN "JANE EYRE"

A similar sensibility emerges in the heroine of Charlotte Brontë's great novel, *Jane Eyre*. Although Jane Eyre is consciously traditionally Christian in her references to a male God-image, whenever she is in serious trouble, it is unconsciously a female God who sustains her. During the desperate privations of Lowood School, for instance, Jane notices the coming of spring, "freshening daily, suggest[ing] the thought that Hope traversed them at night, and left each morning brighter traces of her steps."[3] Tempted to live with the already married Mr. Rochester, Jane is visited at night by a "white human form . . . inclining a glorious brow earth-ward." Speaking to her spirit, this female form of God says, "My daughter, flee temptation!" And Jane replies, "Mother, I will."[4] This vision is an externalization of Jane's inward self-approval and shows her empowering identification with a divine female role model. Running away from Rochester, Jane has "no relative but the universal mother, Nature."[5] And when she is on the verge of giving up control of her life to the coldly ideological St. John Rivers, "nature" sends her another vision to warn her that Rochester is now free to marry her and badly in need of her. As before, the vision comes in the darkness. And Jane muses:

> "Down superstition" . . . as that spectre rose up black by the black yew at the gate. "This is not thy deception, nor thy witchcraft: it is the work of nature. She was roused and did— no miracle—but her best."[6]

No matter that Jane Eyre shortly after this uses a mascu-line pronoun concerning the "Mighty Spirit" to whom she penetrates "very near" in her prayer. Consciously, she is all traditional orthodoxy; but unconsciously, it is Nature as a fe-male deity who intervenes to guide Jane toward wholeness. When Jane marries Rochester, the marriage is between equals because Rochester has lost both his wealth and his eyesight, while Jane has received a legacy not only of money but of her own inner power, the power of autonomous action. As Jane comments after ordering the imperious St. John Rivers out of her presence, "He obeyed at once. Where there is energy to command well enough, obedience never fails."[7]

EMILY BRONTË ON DARKNESS

It is not surprising that the author of *Jane Eyre* thought it important to publish Emily's poem about the power of the earth, the power of nature, after her sister's death. Charlotte Brontë understood that because of their socialization, nineteenth-century Christian women would consciously call God "He," as Jane Eyre did; but she also knew that the divine power was a female, dark, unconscious, earthy power as well as a male, bright, conscious "heavenly" one. And it is the darker manifestation of God-as-female that empowers women.

Emily Brontë wrote a poem in 1845 in which she stated an explicit preference for night, an identification with the stars rather than with the "dazzling sun." It is not farfetched to see in this poem the sun as a symbol of patriarchal power and the stars of the night as symbols of a gentler, more restful power of full humanity (not without light, but without blinding or burning light). The remarkable untitled poem concludes:

> O Stars and Dreams and Gentle Night;
> O Night and Stars return!
> And hide me from the hostile light
> That does not warm, but burn—
>
> That drains the blood of suffering men;
> Drinks tears, instead of dew:
> Let me sleep through his blinding reign;
> And only wake with you![8]

ALICE WALKER, MEDIUM OF THE SPIRIT

In our own day, this type of godding has produced many wonderful works, but none more wonderful than the novel *The Color Purple*, by Alice Walker. (I sometimes worry that the movie of the same name will discourage people from reading the novel. The movie is good enough as a show, but totally misses the gradual process of redemption that is at the heart

of the novel). In the dedication, Alice Walker claims the same
divine inspiration that Milton claimed in *Paradise Lost*: "To
the spirit:/Without whose assistance /Neither this book/Nor
I/Would have been/Written." And just as Milton claimed
his poetry to have been "easy" and "unpremeditated," given
to him by a divine woman in the night, so Alice Walker's epilogue thanks "everybody in this book for coming" and signs
herself "A. W., author and medium." It is gorgeous to see a
young black woman claiming the same powerful connection
to God that white males like John Milton have periodically
felt free to claim!

If indeed the book is a gift of the divine Spirit working
through the medium of Alice Walker's talented spirit—and I
certainly experience the novel that way—I would expect it to
recount a process that moves toward human healing and
wholeness. And that is exactly what I find. Among the redemptive forces that turn Celie from a sexually and violently
abused victim to a radiant lesbian woman who is in charge of
her own life, we find both women and men. Miraculously,
even Albert, who was Celie's abusive husband in his ignorant
days, becomes Celie's good friend by the end of the novel.
Celie writes to Nettie:

> After all the evil he done I know you wonder why I don't hate
> him. I don't hate him for two reasons. One, he love Shug.
> And two, Shug used to love him. Plus, look like he trying to
> make something out of himself. I don't mean just that he
> work and he clean up after himself and he appreciate some of
> the things God was playful enough to make. I mean when
> you talk to him now, he really listen, and one time, out of no-
> where in the conversation us was having, he said Celie, I'm
> satisfied this is the first time I ever lived on Earth as a natural
> man. It feels like a new experience.[9]

Even Albert is godding! As a result of his new birth, he accepts Celie's definition of herself and refuses to join the rest of
society by trivializing her orientation:

Sofia and Harpo always try to set me up with some man. They know I love Shug but they think womens love just by accident, anybody handy likely to do. Every time I go to Harpo's some little policy salesman git all up in my face. Mr.—[Albert] have to come to the rescue. He tell the man, This lady my wife. The man vanish out the door.[10]

Like many feminist men, Albert has to act in a private way to secure for Celie the respect she would naturally be accorded if she were living in an already realized New Creation or New Humanity instead of in a far-from-just and far-from-humane society. He is thus serving Celie's best interests in a way not unrelated to the instruction of Ephesians 5:21: "Be subject to one another out of reverence for Christ."

WALKER'S DEPICTION OF BLACK MEN

Certain black scholars have responded negatively to *The Color Purple*, arguing that Alice Walker has depicted black men as so brutal and irresponsible that she has done a disservice to the black community in a racist society. But surely this is to overlook the combination-portrait Alice Walker has painted of an ideal black man, who would combine the steadiness of Samuel, the self-giving of liberated Albert, the joy of liberated Harpo, the harmlessness of Grady, the unselfishness of Adam (who mutilates his face to identify with his beloved Tasha), and, above all, Jack's ability to be a responsible and loving husband and father. Significantly, it is from a pair of Jack's old army fatigues that Celie makes the first pair of pants in a business venture which ultimately makes her an independent career woman as the head of Folkspants, Unlimited. Celie tries to envision the perfect pair of pants to thank Jack for being the kind of man he is:

Jack is tall and kind and don't hardly say anything. Love children. Respect his wife, Odessa, and all Odessa amazon

sisters. Anything she want to take on, he right there. . . . And
then I remember one time he touch me. And it felt like his
fingers had eyes. Felt like he knew me all over, but he just
touch my arm up near the shoulder.[11]

Celie is lesbian, but like most lesbians, she does not hate men.
And people who accuse Alice Walker of defaming black men
need to learn to read more carefully. No novel that stemmed
from divine-human cooperation would be likely to defame
and demean half of the human race.

FEMINIST MYSTICISM COLORED PURPLE

Did Alice Walker consciously intend to write a book about
godding? Certainly she has not used the term and perhaps
would not care for the term, but just as certainly she has
written a novel about the work of God's reconciling grace being carried out through human agency. Not only do we have
that marvelous dedication and epilogue; we also have a series
of overtly mystical passages in the second half of the novel, as
liberation is occurring. For instance, there is the scene when
Shug Avery is teaching Celie how to rid herself of the white
male image of God that has been so enervating and alienat-
ing to Celie. Predictably enough, after what we have seen in
the Brontës, Shug describes a process of identification with
the divine milieu:

My first step from the old white man was trees. Then air.
Then birds. Then other people. But one day when I was set-
ting quiet and feeling like a motherless child, which I was, it
came to me: that feeling of being part of everything, not separate at all. I knew that if I cut a tree, my arm would bleed.
And I laughed and I cried and I run all around the house. I
knew just what it was. In fact, when it happen, you can't

miss it. It sort of like you know what, she say, grinning and rubbing high up on my thigh.[12]

Shug shocks Celie by describing her mystical experience of oneness with the Creator and the creation in terms of sexual oneness; but mystics have been doing that for centuries! And as a result of that electrifying experience, Shug knows that "God is everything. . . . Everything that is or ever was or ever will be. And when you can feel that, and be happy to feel that, you've found It."

So Shug teaches Celie that God made human sexuality, and loves "Them feelings," and that Celie can "just relax, go with everything that's going, and praise God by liking what you like." And above all, God enjoys admiration, not because God is vain, but because God likes to share a good thing and is just as eager to please human beings as any human being is to please God. Celie asks, "You mean it [God] want to be-loved, just like the Bible say." And Shug replies, "Yes. . . . Everything want to be loved." On the strength of Shug's conviction, Celie begins the long hard process of "Trying to chase that old white man out of my head"[13] in order to empower herself as a black woman.

Later in the novel we find that Celie has succeeded in the empowerment process. She no longer has to smoke reefer in order to feel herself in communion with God; she tells Sophia: "Lately I feel like me and God make love just fine anyhow." When Sophia expresses shock at the sexual metaphor, as Celie had earlier done, Celie assures her, "Girl, I'm bless . . . God know what I mean."[14]

And Nettie, Celie's sister, also has been experiencing God in a life-changing fashion that has made a "godder" out of her.

God is different to us now, after all these years in Africa. More spirit than ever before, and more internal. Most people think he has to look like something or someone—a roofleaf or

Christ—but we don't. And not being tied to what God looks like, frees us.[15]

Nettie is a Christian missionary in Africa, and uses the traditional "he" to refer to God. But we sense that when she comes to America and has the "long talks" with Celie that she is planning on, Celie will help her to see that exclusive use of masculine pronouns concerning God is part of the idolatry Nettie wants freedom from. With her husband, Samuel, Nettie dreams of founding a new church in the black community "that has no idols in it whatsoever, in which each person's spirit is encouraged to seek God directly...."[16] People would go to this church to empower each other to believe that the direct experience of God is possible within the human condition. For as Shug told Celie earlier on, "Any God I ever felt in church I brought in with me. And I think all the other folks did too. They came to church to *share* God, not find God."[17]

What I have called godding, Alice Walker depicts as an earthy, joyous, interactively mutual, full-blooded humanity appreciative of God's love flowing within the creation as well as beyond the limits of any created thing. The God who wants us to notice the color purple is all that human beings imagine, and then some—everything that is or ever was or ever will be. With the confidence that such an "Undying Life" is above me and through me and in me as well as everyone and everything else, moving us all through light and darkness toward complete wholeness, there is no way that I can have a coward soul. Come to think of it, I'd really like to help Nettie and Samuel build their new church!

NOTES

1. *The Norton Anthology of Literature by Women*, ed. Sandra M. Gilbert and Susan Gubar (New York: W. W. Norton, 1985), p. 750. I have added modern punctuation to the poem.

2. Ibid., p. 752.

3. Ibid., p. 411.

4. Ibid., p. 621.

5. Ibid., p. 623.

6. Ibid., p. 707.

7. Ibid.

8. Ibid., p. 748

9. *The Color Purple* (New York: Pocket Books, 1982), p. 230.

10. Ibid.

11. Ibid., p. 191.

12. Ibid., p. 178.

13. Ibid., pp. 178–79.

14. Ibid., p. 197.

15. Ibid., p. 227.

16. Ibid.

17. Ibid., p. 176.

Appendix:
Some Biblical Passages
That Imply Godding

To have discussed each of these passages at length in the text would have been tedious for those readers who are not as enthusiastic about the Bible as I am. But here are citations of some passages I noticed particularly on my most recent "read through" of the Hebrew and Christian Scriptures, along with my comments on them. The list is far from definitive.

Genesis 1:28 — God voluntarily self-limits God's transcendent power by giving responsibility to human beings for the stewardship and governing of the earth.

Psalm 82:6–7 — Human beings (rulers) are gods, offspring of the Most High, but fall into death because they have failed to do justice.

Psalm 119:32, 37, 40 — My running, God's path; my life, God's work; my life renewed in God's righteousness.

Isaiah 2:17	The arrogance of "separated" egotism/pride will be humbled; the Sovereign (the whole of All Reality) will be exalted.
Isaiah 30:21	Human beings who are open to it receive guidance from beyond themselves.
Isaiah 42:1	God's Spirit is "on" the righteous servant.
Isaiah 58:6–10	Human beings who do justice are glorified with the Sovereign's own glory.
Jeremiah 22:16	Defending the cause of the poor and needy is the very *meaning* of "knowing God."
Jeremiah 20:9	God's word can burn in a human heart and in human bones.
John 10:35	Those to whom God's word came are called gods.
John 13:20	Whoever accepts Jesus' messenger accepts Jesus.
John 14:12–14	Believers will do even greater works than Jesus, who will do whatever they ask in Jesus' name.
John 15:4–7	Jesus is *in* the believer and the believer is *in* Jesus.

John 16:14–15	What belongs to God the Father and Mother, belongs to Jesus; what belongs to Jesus is given to believers by the Spirit.
John 17:21	Our being is *in* the divine Parent and Child as the Parent is *in* the Child and the Child is *in* the Parent. This is the proof for the world that God sent Jesus.
Acts 6:8	Stephen was full of God's grace and power.
Romans 2:10	Glory, honor, and peace for *everyone* who does good.
Romans 8:28–29	God works for human good within every circumstance ("good" and "bad"); and the Christ was firstborn among *many* sisters and brothers.
1 Corinthians 12:6–11	God actually does all that God's servants do. All human spiritual gifts are the work of the Holy Spirit.
1 Corinthians 12:25, 27	Believers are Christ's body; all parts should have equal concern for each other.
Ephesians 4:15	People of faith are to grow up into the Head (into fully adult Christedness).
Ephesians 4:24	Believers put on a new self, "created to be like God in true righteousness and holiness."

Hebrews 2:11	Holy human beings are God's family, Jesus' sisters and brothers.
I Peter 1:15	Human beings are to be holy as God is holy.
I Peter 4:10	Everybody is instructed to administer God's grace in its various forms by serving other people.
II Peter 1:4	Through God's promises, human beings participate in the divine nature.
1 John 4:12–13	If human beings love each other, God is living in them, and God's love is perfected (completed) in them. In fact, not only does God live in human beings; they also live in God; and the proof is God's own Spirit given to humankind.

And others!